# FIVE STAR LOVE

## HOW TO TREAT YOUR TRUE LOVE LIKE A CUSTOMER AND GET THE MARRIAGE OF YOUR DREAMS

DENNIS GREEN & MARY LOU GREEN

Boulevard Press

# FIVE STAR LOVE

How to Treat Your True Love Like a Customer
and Get the marriage of Your Dreams

Copyright © 2018 Dennis Green & Mary Lou Green

All Rights Reserved.

ISBN-13: 978-0-9832411-6-4

ISBN-10: 0-893241163

Learn more about the authors on our websites at:

DennisAndMaryLou.com  or  BigIdeaSchool.com

Boulevard Press

# We Want to Hear Your Love Story

Contact us here:
DennisAndMaryLou.com

*Dennis & Mary Lou*

## Dedication

For Mary Lou's parents,

Bob and Mary Ann Wickens,

and their 60 years together.

Thanks for showing us what true love is.

# Acknowledgments

To Dennis and Kathleen for showing us that love is alive and well and filled with promise. To Pat and Teri for loving each other and showing it every day. To Jon and Sharon for making love work. To Bob and Felice for showing us that love is filled with surprise. To Charles and Hilary for proving love is joyful and constant. To Kae and Peter for their passion and loving friendship. To Joe and Joan for showing us that love survives tragedy. To Larry and Gege for showing how love heals. To Karla and Dan for proving that love works no matter how often you move. To Jim and Patti, Bob and Jan, Jim and Heather, Benson and Lou, Dick and Mary, Morris and Connie, Frank and Phyllis, Janice and Larry, Elmo and Jeri, Tom and Barb, and Ron and Annie for showing that love lasts.

Additional thanks to Karla Hawley for her passionate, skillful editing and for reminding us that absolutes are few and that there are many kinds of relationships in this changing world.

Special thanks to the many professionals whose work helped us navigate the complex workings of love, marriage and customer care. They include: John M. Gottman, Ph.D., Dr. Emmerson Eggerichs, Ph.D., Louann Brizendine, M.D., Martin E.P. Seligman, Ph.D., Edward T. Hall, Dr. Ellen Wachtel Ph.D., Michele Weiner Davis, Scott Haltzman, M.D., Theresa Foy Digeronimo, M.Ed., John Friel, PhD., Linda Friel, M.A., Mark Goulston M.D. John Gray, Ph.D., John R. Dijulius III, Tony Hsieh, Leonardo Inghilleri, Micah Solomon, Danny Meyer, Al Ritter, Arielle Ford, Charles Duhigg, John Murphy, Francis Cole Jones, Howard Shultz, Carl Sewell, Jeffrey Gitomer. Any mistakes or misinterpretations of their work are strictly our responsibility.

# Table of Contents

# A New Way to Stay in Love

What makes this book about relationships different from those written by psychologists, pastors and marriage counselors is this: we are entrepreneurs. What do we know about marriage? We have been married for 39 years and have worked together as entrepreneurs even longer.

People often ask us how we manage to work together every day in our business inventing consumer products and still remain so much in love. We'll begin with a story that inspired us to write *Five Star Love*.

**Dennis:** Some years ago, Mary Lou and I were playing golf together. We stopped our cart near a hole, and when Mary Lou reached for the chipping wedge in her bag, she discovered she had left it on a previous green. My first thought was to let her backtrack and look for the club on her own so she would learn to manage her equipment. I worried this was slowing us down and holding up the group trailing us, so I gave her my wedge to use and implied

I could find her lost club faster than she could. I said I would catch up with her and the other twosome on the next tee box. Retrieving her club reminded me of a golf game I'd recently played with one of our customers. He also had left a club behind, but in his case I recalled acting and feeling quite differently.

As soon as my customer mentioned the missing club, I jumped into my cart and assured him I'd take care of it. Did I imply or even think he was holding us up or suggest he needed to better manage his equipment? No! Did I tell him I could find his club faster than he could? No! I just wanted to be sure he enjoyed the game. I didn't want him to worry about anything. That was when it hit me. If Mary Lou were my customer, I wouldn't assume she needed a lesson in managing her equipment or that she wasn't capable of retrieving her own club. I love Mary Lou deeply and certainly more than any customer, but I suddenly realized I wasn't acting like it. I was being a complete jerk.

## RIDING BACK TO CATCH UP WITH MARY LOU, I HAD AN EPIPHANY THAT WOULD CHANGE MY LIFE AND OUR MARRIAGE…FOREVER.

When I caught up with our group, I dropped Mary Lou's club in her bag but didn't tell her about my realization. She thanked me for helping and said she wished I had gotten to finish the hole, too. She was more worried about my feelings than her own. That's the way she is.

That golf incident made me wonder how I was making Mary Lou feel every day. Was I acting like a dope for a long time and didn't know it? I recalled reading somewhere how a woman doesn't want to hear the gory details about how her knight has slain the dragon. She wants to hear he did it for her. I wished I had said to her, "I don't want you to feel rushed. Let me find your club so you can keep playing. I don't need to finish this hole." If I had said that, she would have known I was slaying the dragon for her, not for me.

That night I laid awake worrying about how I had treated the love of my life. I wasn't proud of myself. In fact I was ashamed. If you are having problems in your relationship, you might wonder why I was so worked up over a misplaced golf club. But my concern went much deeper than this one incident.

I was married the first time at age 19 to Karen, my high school sweetheart. Less than two years after our wedding, she died in the hospital after a routine gall bladder operation. It was the most painful experience of my life, and it's still extremely tough to talk about or even think about a half-century later.

Our son was seven months old and I was a sophomore in college. When I graduated, I married again. That lasted seven years before ending in divorce. Mary Lou is my third marriage, so I was keenly aware of what could go wrong if I neglected to show how much I cared for her.

### EACH TIME YOU HAVE A SMALL POSITIVE MOMENT WITH YOUR PARTNER, YOU BUILD EQUITY IN YOUR RELATIONSHIP. THE TINIEST NEGATIVE MOMENT CHIPS AWAY PIECES OF THAT EQUITY.

I've seen complacency creep into other marriages and experienced failure myself. Indifference sneaks up on you. One day you are deeply in love and suddenly you're drowning in disappointment and don't understand how you got there. You don't lose your love for each other in one instant, though. Changes often take years to develop. New love strikes like lightning, but seasoned love can sneak away in the dead of night, so quietly that you hardly notice—until it's gone. Every moment you have with your partner or your customer makes a subconscious impression. As Malcolm Gladwell shows in his book

*The Tipping Point*, "Little things make a big difference."

You don't notice how you gradually stop complimenting your partner or quit helping each other around the house. You don't turn down the bed covers or kiss each other goodnight or hug before you leave for work. You disagree about what the kids should eat or when they should go to bed. Irritations morph into animosity. You stop listening to each other about a problem at work or something troubling you regarding the kids.

When big things come along such as an affair, the death of a child, the loss of a job or business, or a foreclosure on your home, you blame each other. Little by little your love dissolves and you wonder what happened.

When you truly love someone, as I love Mary Lou, a little problem may feel like a pebble in your shoe. It won't kill you, but it still hurts and the longer it remains, the worse it feels.

> ### BAD RELATIONSHIPS DON'T APPEAR OUT OF THE BLUE. EMOTIONAL ROCKS PILE UP UNTIL YOU REALIZE IT'S NOT YOUR FOOT THAT HURTS, IT'S YOUR HEART.

Mary Lou's lost golf club was my wake-up call. I realized I had been more concerned about my customer's needs than about hers. Maybe it was because showing my customer a good time would result in more sales, so it felt like there was more at stake if I lost him—though I can't imagine any relationship more vital than my marriage to Mary Lou or how devastating it would be to lose her. That's when I understood how much I was taking her for granted. I needed to change, to bring the same urgency I felt for her when we fell in love. I needed her to feel that she was everything to me.

Then this crazy idea occurred to me. What if I imagined Mary Lou was my customer—as a way of reminding me what was at stake in our relationship. At first, that sounded nuts. And yet, comparing her needs to my customer's needs is the very thing that woke me up. Maybe the customer analogy would help me stay awake. I decided to tell Mary Lou what I was feeling and to apologize for the way I had treated her.

# Applying Customer Care to Marriage

*Mary Lou:* When Dennis told me what happened on the golf course, and explained his customer analogy, we talked about his feelings and our relationship. At that time, we had been married for 30 years (now 39). In examining our comfortable routine, we realized something was missing. We weren't questioning our commitment for one another, but we worried about drifting apart as we had seen so many other couples do.

## WE HAD NEVER THOUGHT ABOUT THE CONNECTION BETWEEN CUSTOMER CARE IN BUSINESS AND CARING FOR EACH OTHER.

We kicked around what would happen if we thought of each other as customers, the kind we loved being around and working with, not the toxic kind that were hard to tolerate. Customers can also be abusive, and we didn't want to model that kind of relationship. Would this customer concept heighten our awareness and help us find ways to reward each other? Would it feel mechanical and unromantic? Would it kill spontaneity and make love feel calculated? Would it lead to keeping score, something neither of us believed in or practiced? We wondered. On the other hand, our business over the past 30 years was about inventing new products, so why not try a new way to stay in love?

When you think about it, dating is like caring for a VIP customer. You provide the ultimate in customer service. You want to learn everything you can about this fabulous human being at the center of your universe. No detail is insignificant. You spend hours thinking about what you can do to make the relationship better. Every comment is significant. Every glance holds meaning. You spend hours figuring out how you are alike and how you are different. Will the relationship feel this good tomorrow, next week, next month?

Granted, talking about customer care may not sound romantic, but the more we talked about being customers of each other, the more we realized how much romance is also sparked by the same values customers care about. Great companies use these values to build brand loyalty including: respect, fair treatment, trust, loyalty, reciprocation and fulfilment.

Could this customer analogy make us more conscious of each other's needs? Was it possible that this simple idea would ignite renewed interest in one another? Would it really help us see one another in new ways? We decided to give it a try. The first week was an experiment, and we were hyper-alert about finding ways to surprise and reward one another. It almost became a competition as love notes appeared in unexpected places and chores were done without reminders. We found ourselves smiling more and hugging more and remembering what it was like to put one another first before anyone or anything else. It felt like we were dating again.

## Great Service Sparks Romance

We already loved each other deeply, but we had no idea how much more we could learn about how to show it. As we continued to up our level of customer care, we became even more conscious of each other's needs and how to fulfill them. Within a few months, we both felt that becoming customers of each other took us to a higher level of understanding, appreciation and love. It had become a welcome habit. We didn't have to think about how to care—we automatically became more caring.

> **TREATING ONE ANOTHER AS CUSTOMERS STIMULATED US TO DISCOVER PRACTICAL WAYS TO CARE THAT WE HAD NEVER CONSCIOUSLY CONSIDERED.**

## Why We Wrote This Book

To our knowledge no one has used the customer analogy to shine a light on marriage and use it to develop positive habits that will keep your marriage growing. Our customer analogy is like a mnemonic, a reminder that helps you develop caring into a positive habit. To make this process work, however, we discovered we had to think and act as equal customers of each other, and understand that some days or even weeks, one of us required more care than the other.

Choice is power. You can choose to dissolve bad habits and create new positive ones. You can satisfy your partner and keep them happy or disappoint them and lose them out of carelessness and neglect. In the process of writing *Five Star Love*, it surprised us how the habit of showing our love turned the routine of everyday living, what we call the "business side of marriage," into unlimited opportunities for sharing our love and feeling romance. Eight years ago we started writing down what we were learning about our customer approach.

This is what we did to bring our idea to life. First, we studied the works of top psychologists, relationship counselors, marriage therapists and church pastors. Next, we looked at the best practices from successful world-class customer service programs and examined the theories of how habits are formed and changed.

Finally, we included our own personal experience from 39 years of marriage and working with customers from around the world. To make our idea useful, we distilled everything into what we call *The Ten Habits of Passionate Customer Care.*

## WE'RE CONFIDENT THAT WHEN YOU INTERNALIZE THESE TEN HABITS AND APPLY THEM TO YOUR RELATIONSHIP, YOU WILL GET THE MARRIAGE OF YOUR DREAMS.

We wrote this book together, and generally with one combined voice. We also speak in our individual voices. When **Mary Lou** is speaking, you will see her name in bold italics at the beginning of the paragraph, and likewise for **Dennis.**

### Final Note:

*Five Star Love* does not address serious marital problems involving drug or spousal abuse, divorce, infidelity, child abuse and other complex issues for which professional psychologists and therapists are trained. We also don't discuss how children fit into this habit-forming process. That deserves a book of its own. Our spotlight focuses on couples. We believe, however, that when children witness their parents genuinely caring for each other, they can't help but also benefit and build positive habits of their own.

We are not psychologists or marriage counselors. We are entrepreneurs experienced in caring for each other and addressing customer needs.

## OUR PURPOSE IS TO HELP YOU DEVELOP HABITS AND SKILLS THAT BUILD MUTUAL LOVE, LOYALTY, TRUST AND RESPECT.

We hope *Five Star Love* gives you a new way to think about your relationship. Love begins with showing how much you care for each other. Right now is a great time to demonstrate your love. Don't wait. Start today to develop caring habits. You will never come in second when you are the first to care.

May you stay in love forever,

*Dennis and Mary Lou*

# WHY WE NEED TO BE REMINDED TO CARE

Long-term success in business comes from consistently delivering great product and following it up with superior customer care. This also happens to be a prescription for staying in love.

A business that doesn't listen to its customers, doesn't innovate and doesn't keep ahead of its competition, is likely to limp along keeping its head above water until it finally fails.

Likewise, your marriage will fail if you don't show how much you care about your sweetheart—your customer. Success comes from keeping your customer relationship fresh and growing while understanding that competition for the attention of your soulmate abounds.

Nobody likes a lackluster product or poor customer care at the store or at home. What really matters is making your true love feel they got a great deal when they picked you. Out of all the choices they've had, or might have in the future, you want them to say they would pick you again and be your partner for life.

## IF YOU DON'T GIVE YOUR PARTNER WHAT THEY NEED, THEY CAN ALWAYS SHOP ELSEWHERE, IF ONLY IN THEIR MIND.

When you treat your partner badly, bits of loyalty can drift away to unseen rivals, or to friends or family members, who will listen and commiserate about marital disappointments. In business and in personal relationships, complacency is an indifferent devil.

You can live together for a lifetime and still lose each other by not paying attention. Succeeding at love is not a question of doing the minimum to reduce complaints. It's about delighting your treasured customer.

Passionate customer care requires imagination and a commitment to action to prove you care more than just a little. You must care beyond your partners' expectations. It's not enough to tell yourself you love your partner. You need to consistently demonstrate it. Adequate care is not enough. You need to show *passionate* care.

You have probably heard the saying, "familiarity breeds contempt." Familiarity also breeds complacency and carelessness. The longer you live together the less you think of your partner as a heavenly being. Acting natural and open with each other is a good thing, but in the process you can also lose the romance and the mystery that's so much a part of falling in love. The question is how to hold on to the excitement and romance so vital to a long and healthy marriage. One cue or trigger we started using is what we call our Customer Mantra because it is such a powerful reminder for how to treat one another. Regardless of the situation, but especially in moments of potential conflict, we would say this Customer Mantra in our heads.

## WOULD I SAY THAT TO A CUSTOMER?

The more we used the Customer Mantra the better we felt about each other and ourselves. We realized repeating this mantra until it became a habit made us feel more loved, and more loving.

## Love from a Customer's Point of View

Anyone who has owned or managed a business realizes how important it is to keep customers happy, but not everyone has run a business or had to care for customers. You might be concerned that thinking of your soulmate as a customer devalues them. You may believe that you treat your partner better than any customer. Some people in business even resent customers and feel they are merely a necessary evil. For them, customers can be demanding or even abusive, so asking them to think of their sweetheart as a customer feels wrong.

But we have all been customers, clients, patients or students so let's look at love from that point of view and see how the Customer Mantra fosters empathy. We all know what it feels like to be a valued customer. We also know how it feels to be treated badly. We have all been disappointed by the bad service endured at restaurants, dry cleaners, or even hospitals, so when we are treated with extraordinary care, we treasure the experience and make it a point to tell anyone who will listen. Likewise, we broadcast bad service even louder because carelessness breeds resentment and anger.

### WE ALL CRAVE TO BE TREATED IN WAYS THAT SHOW WE MATTER.

No doubt you think you treat your sweetheart well, but what do they think? You may think you are God's gift to the relationship, and already do a magnificent job of caring. But does your partner share that opinion? If you did a lover satisfaction survey the way a good company evaluates customer satisfaction, would you find out you aren't as caring as you think?

Extraordinary customer care makes us feel respected. We also feel a bond of friendship and loyalty with someone who shows they truly understand and care about our needs. What's more, great care motivates us to reciprocate care, and that is where we truly profit as a couple. When you treat someone well, the chances are very good they will treat you well in return.

We all have days when nothing is going right and feel the last thing we need to worry about is someone else's needs. This is the very time we need to demonstrate care. Imagining each other as customers works especially well in stressful moments when we feel a conflict coming on and want to lash out and say something we will regret. In times like these we can stop and silently call up the Customer Mantra. It's so important it bears repeating.

## Would i say that to a customer?

This question helps us pause before reacting. It helps us remember that disrespected partners, like dissatisfied customers, can take their loyalties across the street or down the block to someone who does care. The mental image of them "packing up their heart" and returning it to the store, or giving it away to someone else, reminds us that love and loyalty need to be earned every day and are easily lost through rudeness, abuse and apathy.

In our company, we worked hard to win our customers and knew how easily we could lose them if we stopped caring about their needs. We regret losing some because we didn't show them how much they mattered. Many of the business examples we use in the book are taken from this personal customer experience.

Caring can't be turned on like a lamp; however, empathy and care can be learned and practiced and become a positive habit. Showing each other you care will inspire intimacy and romantic desire no matter what age you are or how long you have been married or in a committed relationship. The Ten Habits of Passionate Customer Care in the chapters ahead reveal how to care passionately and how to get what you want from marriage by fulfilling your partner's needs. We hope these ten habits will recharge you each day and help you show each other you aren't taking anything for granted.

Before we go into detail about how to develop The Ten Habits of Passionate Customer Care, we want to show you why they are necessary and why we believe they will work to ignite passion in your relationship.

In the next chapter we will state the case for why many marriages fail, and how customer care works as a preventative medicine to keep love alive.

# WHY MARRIAGES FAIL

People who feel unhappy in their marriages often gripe, "What happened to the romance we had when we were dating?" Here is how one woman put it: "Before we were married he sent me flowers and little notes. He held my hand all the time. We went to concerts. We danced. We went out to dinner and talked for hours and he seemed to care about what I thought. Now we argue about money and the kids. He comes home later and later from work. He plays games on his computer and we hardly see each other. This is not what I thought marriage would be like."

A man described his marriage this way: "She's not the same woman she was when we were dating. I'd pick her up to go out, and she looked like a million bucks. She was in great shape. Now she's put on a lot of weight and wears sweatshirts and baggy pants to hide it. Her hair used to be long and silky. Now it's almost as short as mine. In the beginning, she would tell me how smart I was. Now I'm the dumbest guy on the planet. She never complained about little things before. She was always positive. Now nothing seems to be good enough for her. I can't do anything right. I don't make enough money. I work too much. I don't spend enough time with the kids—and when I do, I let them get away with too much. Being married is not what I call fun."

The list of reasons people give for why their marriages failed include the usual suspects: financial problems, infidelity, in-laws, and disagreements about how to raise the kids. None of these are the true reasons why marriages fall apart. We believe these problems are merely the symptoms of something more fundamental.

## MARRIAGES FAIL FOR THE SAME REASON BUSINESSES FAIL. THEY STOP SHOWING THEIR CUSTOMERS THAT THEY CARE.

If that sounds too simple, think back to when you started shopping at a new store or eating at a new restaurant. At the grand opening, you were treated like a rich relative. Now recall when you started dating and treated each other like royalty. You didn't argue then about little things that bothered you. You were too busy loving each other. Even the big things didn't seem insurmountable because you believed your love could get you through anything.

The store or the restaurant that continued their royal treatment is likely still in business and doing well. How about the ones that took their customers for granted? *Five Star Love* is a reminder that caring is not a one-time event. It's an ongoing process that must be practiced daily until it becomes second nature.

It may seem like a chicken or egg problem. Do we stop caring because of problems, or do problems overwhelm us because we stop caring? We believe the latter, that problems engulf us because we have stopped caring about each other and that isolates us and makes us feel alone. Together we can endure anything. Alone, the smallest troubles can feel too much to bear. The bumps we were able to glide over in the beginning loom like mountains ahead when we have no one to share the journey. No business can succeed by taking a day off from treating its customers well. Imagine a sign on the front door of your favorite coffee shop or restaurant that announced:

### TODAY WE DON'T CARE ABOUT YOU.

You can't stay in love by implying that some days your partner doesn't matter. Marriages fail because caring fails. By demonstrating care every day, you share preventative medicine that binds you together to face the problems that threaten to unravel your marriage.

## Rewards Motivate Us to Care

We treat each other well for the same reasons that motivate companies to care for their customers. In a word, it's about "rewards." Company employees are motivated to treat customers well so they will buy more. The company makes a profit and the employees get rewarded through recognition and bonuses. When customers feel cared for, they return and make new purchases to continue the virtuous cycle of reciprocal care and reward.

### IT IS HUMAN NATURE TO CARE MORE ABOUT SOMETHING THAT OFFERS A REWARD. HOW ARE YOU REWARDING EACH OTHER?

As children, we earn an allowance by cleaning our rooms and doing chores around the house. Belonging to the Boy Scouts or Girl Scouts offers the chance to earn merit badges by achieving certain goals. In school we get gold stars, ribbons and trophies for doing well. What is the payoff for married partners to treat each other well? We could list sex, security, companionship, children and emotional support. But these incentives, other than sex (and that depends on who feels rewarded), are not as measurable or as tangible as purchase orders, merit badges, money awards, stock options or promotions.

## Why Do We Stop Rewarding Each Other?

In the dating stage, we pursue our partners with enormous energy, doing everything possible to win them over. The romance stage of a relationship provides intense physical pleasure. The "infatuation high" is a powerful reward. But once the deal is sealed, we often take our partners for granted and neglect to follow through with the brand of service that delivers on our promises of everlasting love.

Marketing guru Harvey MacKay says, "There's a place in the world for any business that takes care of its customers—after the sale." The same can be said of any relationship we care about. Unfortunately, marital benefits are dulled by complacency. Even sex can lose its allure if it becomes a duty or is curtailed because of children's demands, job stress, age, illness or physical changes.

> ### SOME YEARS INTO MARRIAGE BLIND LOVE REGAINS ITS SIGHT, AND WE COME UNDER ATTACK BY THE ROUTINE BUSINESS SIDE OF MARRIAGE.

Studies show problems between couples often arise during a time of transition from romance to "nomance." The perfect bliss enjoyed in our dating years is dampened by the business of household chores, paying bills, raising kids and earning a living. While these are necessary, they hardly provide the same reward as a first kiss or seeing each other naked for the first time. In fact, neuroscientists have shown we actually get a chemical jolt from falling in love, and this love chemistry is both a blessing and a curse.

Our chemistry draws us together, but when the halo effect fades we are left wondering what happened. We feel like something has changed. We change, our partners change, life changes and love changes, often because we stop paying attention and stop caring.

There's truth to the notion that people can become addicted to love. Romantic partners, especially in the first six months, crave the ecstatic feeling of being together and may feel helplessly dependent on each other.

"The classic symptoms of falling in love are similar to the initial effects of taking drugs," writes Louann Brizendine, MD, brain researcher, wife, mother, and author of *The Female Brain* and *The Male Brain*. She says her own brain research and that done by other scientists demonstrates how the excitement we feel when we are extremely attracted to another person is very much like the high induced by drugs like heroin, morphine and OxyContin. She states, "Research into brain chemistry shows how narcotics trigger the brain's reward circuit, causing chemical releases and effects similar to those of romance. Studies of passionate love show this brain state lasts for roughly six to eight months. It is such an intense feeling that our partner's best interest, well-being and survival become as important as, or more important than, one's own."

### START-UP LOVE IS ABOUT DOING EVERYTHING YOU CAN TO WIN YOUR TRUE LOVE'S HEART. STAYING IN LOVE IS ABOUT DOING EVERY-THING YOU CAN TO KEEP IT.

In the process of falling in love, we have no reason to think our ecstasy will ever end. During start-up love, we aren't thinking at all. Our brains are awash in neurotransmitters and hormones that prevent us from considering the future responsibilities of a long-term relationship. When chemicals that support our obsession diminish, sustainable love is put to the test. If we are to stay together and more importantly, stay in love, we need something to bolster our feelings when our hearts fall back to earth.

What do we do when the passion recedes and our judgmental brains awaken from slumber? This is a dangerous period of time when love flourishes or fails. In the business world this transition is analogous to the challenge that a new enterprise faces as it evolves from start-up stage into a going concern filled with mind-numbing details. A business launched on a big idea will only succeed in the long run by keeping customers consistently happy. Succeeding at love requires a commitment to "going-concern behavior," a renewed focus on ways to innovate and show love over time.

## Passionate Care Is the Replacement Drug

Sustaining love is a matter of stimulating brain chemistry after the wedding, after the kids, after the new house and after the daily routine numbs us down. We don't have to let love die a slow death. The natural brain chemistry that juiced us up at the onset of romance doesn't have to be lost as we settle into negotiating the details of living together.

> WE STRESS INNOVATION IN BUSINESSES.
> WE NEED TO DO THE SAME IN
> OUR MARRIAGES.

Romantic love can be maintained through every stage of your marriage—if you develop caring habits and know how to reward one another. The Customer Mantra is a small habit that helps you sustain romantic love by reminding you to care. It's a memory mechanism that stimulates you to care and makes you feel better when you show your partner how much they matter. When you consider your own customer experiences—how you are treated and cared for by others—you know which treatment delights and which discourages, what surprises and what bores, what feels like a reward or a punishment. Passionate care is about making your partner feel wanted the way a business enterprise delights you by going the extra mile to serve your needs.

You may never feel the infatuation high you felt in the beginning of your relationship, but you can express deep, consummate love through passionate caring. You can maintain a different kind of high by finding new opportunities to demonstrate your love and to keep it alive and growing.

Successful companies spend substantial amounts of money on research and development to bring new and innovative products to market. You need to make the same commitment to keeping love fresh by consistently bringing new ways of caring to your relationship. We heard someone say that a couple they knew, who had been married for many years, had fallen in love all over again. How does this awakening happen? Is it as simple as refurbishing a house that has fallen into disrepair? Like a home can be restored and even expanded, so can love be renewed through passionate rewards. The key to restarting love is a matter of focusing on your partner's (customer's) needs.

### IF YOU BEHAVE TOWARD EACH OTHER IN LOVING WAYS, YOUR HEARTS AND MINDS WILL FOLLOW.

Focusing your behavior on caring acts can change how you feel about each other. You can fall in love with the same person again and again by acting as you did when you were falling in love. One man asked us, "But what if I don't feel the same way now as I did back then?" The magic of passionate caring awakens dormant emotions. The feelings kick-started by hormones can be restarted by restoring care.

## Passionate Care Sustains Love

Anyone who has experienced the pulsing heartbeat of "love at first sight," knows the awesome power of physical attraction. But where does it go from there? The attractive stranger that catches your eye from across a crowded room may turn out to be completely opposed to your own deeply held beliefs about family, politics, religion, sports or whatever else you care about. Too often you have nothing in common to support a relationship. Moreover, you might discover they couldn't care less about your feelings or needs.

Infatuation often dies a quick death without the prospect of intimacy. Likewise, a relationship sparked by a common interest or a commitment to a common purpose may feel intimate but never generate any sparks. People who feel no physical attraction can't necessarily become romantically interested in each other by demonstrating passionate care, but if love exists, passionate care can sustain it.

## ACTING IN LOVING WAYS MAKES YOU MORE LOVING—AND MORE LOVABLE.

## We Learn How to Care by Caring

Candidates appearing on the TV show *The Biggest Loser* are a testimony to the power of how changes in behavior can change motivation. When contestants commit to an exercise program and a new diet, they dramatically lose weight. As they are weighed and measured to evaluate progress toward their goal, their body image transforms along with their attitude, shifting radically from negative to positive.

Their results vividly demonstrate how changing their behavior can transform how they feel. It follows that acting in caring ways can make us more caring. Athletes build their stamina through physical exertion. Surgeons enhance their powers by operating. Teachers hone their skills by teaching. Lovers stay in love by demonstrating their love through passionate care. The Ten Habits of Passionate Customer Care presented in the chapters ahead will help you show your partner how much you care.

## Why Not Just Follow The Golden Rule?

The Golden Rule tells us: "Do unto others as you would have them do unto you." This sage advice has guided generations, and we all assume we know what it means. Yet, if we take the words literally, we can uncover a different meaning, one that makes us rethink how we should practice the rule. For example, a literal application of The Golden Rule implies that if you like a glass of wine for dinner, you would "do the same unto others," or believe it was proper to serve them a glass of wine as well. But what if your guest, your sweetheart, or your customer doesn't drink wine or is allergic to alcohol, or drinking violates their religious beliefs? Do your unique desires make it reasonable to expect others to want the same? If you are nuts about science and math, that's hardly a reason to give someone with no interest in math a book about chaos theory—no matter how much *you* enjoy math.

## The Customer Rule

***Dennis:*** Of course, the spirit of The Golden Rule is to encourage you not to treat others badly, but taken literally it implies that others want the same things you want. *The Customer Rule* is different. It declares, "Do unto others according to their needs, not yours."

It follows that you must learn what your customer needs. Before Mary Lou and I started inventing products and managing our marketing company, I was an architect and Mary Lou was an elementary school teacher. Both professions were about satisfying customer needs. As an architect, I spent many hours interviewing my clients. I wasn't merely interested in the spaces they wanted. I had to know how they lived and worked together.

Architects can feel conflicted about trying to satisfy their own artistic needs while honoring their client's creative ideas and functional requirements. Like a married couple, the architect's needs and the client's needs are not always in sync. It takes creative cooperation to satisfy both. When I was an architect, I had to accept the client's needs, not mine, as paramount.

## WHEN YOU ACCEPT THE RESPONSIBILITY OF CONSIDERING YOUR CUSTOMER'S NEEDS FIRST, IT'S EASIER TO SEE HOW TO CARE FOR THEM.

*Mary Lou:* As an elementary teacher, I cared about the needs of my students, parents, principal, administration and school board. Their needs often conflicted or were hard for them to articulate. I also had my own professional and creative needs, including some deeply held convictions about how children learn and the best way to teach them according to their own learning styles and potential. Every year brought new students, new parents and often a new administration embracing a new educational philosophy. In the end, it was all about the students. Their needs were the most important.

The Customer Rule affirms that each customer is different and yearns to be cared for in their own way. It's no different for a husband and wife who must resolve conflicting needs. When you care about each other's best interest, it gets easier to modify your own needs.

It's easy to delude yourself into thinking some things are more urgent than staying in love. But in marriage, love is fundamental to your existence. When you believe you are so right about something your partner must concede, you aren't caring. No matter how much you know about a problem, or how to solve it, you won't succeed if you don't actively demonstrate you care as much about your partner's needs as you do your own.

The remainder of this book is about developing your Ten Habits of Passionate Customer Care and how to apply them in your everyday actions. These habits detail the many different ways you can reward

your partner, ways that you may have never have consciously considered but which may seem obvious when you hear them. Thinking
of your partner as a customer will help you feel the urgency needed
to maintain the feelings of attraction and passion you felt when you
first fell in love.

# The Ten Habits of Passionate Customer Care

In his marvelous book, *The Power of Habit: Why We Do What We Do In Life and Business,* author Charles Duhigg says the process of developing a habit involves a three-step loop. "First, there is a *cue,* a trigger that tells your brain to go into automatic mode and which habit to use. Then there is the *routine,* which can be physical or mental or emotional. Finally, there is the *reward,* which helps your brain figure out if this particular loop is worth remembering. Over time this loop—cue, routine, reward; cue, routine, reward becomes more and more automatic. The cue and reward become intertwined until a powerful sense of anticipation and craving emerges. Eventually, whether in a chilly MIT laboratory or your driveway, a habit is born."

You might say that this habit loop represents the underlying process of married life. You have a problem, a need or a request. That becomes a *cue.* Your partner helps you solve the problem and that's a *routine.* The *reward* is a reciprocation such as a thank you, a hug, a mention to family members about how great you are, a note on your pillow or a thousand other forms of gratitude. Habits can be good or bad. Bad ones are hard to break and good ones take practice and repetition to create. Practicing a routine, again and again, builds muscle and mental memory that takes over the process. The remainder of *Five Star Love* shows you how to develop the habits that will help you make the marriage of your dreams.

The next ten chapters will help you get in the habit of caring for each other. You will see examples of how to care and do practice exercises and take a self-administered test to help you evaluate how well you are caring for your partner. Here are the ten habits *Five Star Love* will help you develop:

## THE TEN HABITS OF PASSIONATE CUSTOMER CARE

1. ASSESSMENT
2. PREPARATION
3. RESPECT
4. RECIPROCATION
5. ENGAGEMENT
6. EXPECTATIONS
7. FAIRNESS
8. TRUST
9. ROMANCE
10. PERSONAL CARE

1. ASSESSMENT: How much do you know about each other's true needs? This habit helps you think about and identify your true love's needs. Continuously assessing each other's needs fosters empathy, tempers your emotions and makes you aware of changes in your relationship.

2. PREPARATION: Are you prepared to care with the same effort you want to be cared for? This habit makes you ready to overcome the discomforts and annoyances that make you angry with one another. It helps you serve each other's needs and recognize the many opportunities you have to demonstrate care.

3. RESPECT: Do you respect each other? This habit helps you value one another's interests, ideas, and intelligence, and understand their fears, viewpoints and motives. You draw on this habit to support their desires, worries and judgments. When you respect and nurture these qualities in yourself, you demonstrate your love and appreciation for your partner as they are, not as you wish they were.

4. RECIPROCATION: Do you know how to give back, to return the good care you receive? This habit helps you develop the capacity to appreciate what your partner does for you and to show it. Reciprocation is not about keeping score; it's about caring in return. When your partner does something for you, draw on this habit to give back and maintain equity in your relationship.

5. ENGAGEMENT: How much of your time do you give your partner? This habit helps you truly connect with each other, not letting the demands of job and family pull you apart. This habit keeps love fresh and exciting. Each time you engage each other with loving words, by touch and with physical gifts, you prove that you like being together.

6. EXPECTATIONS: Do you give the minimal amount of energy to your marriage, or do you exceed your partner's expectations? This habit builds your desire to do more than your partner expects of you. It gives you the ability to surprise and delight your partner by giving more to them than you ask for yourself.

**7. FAIRNESS:** Do you play fair with your partner or take advantage of them? Are you doing your part, carrying your load? This habit makes you aware of your role as a member of team marriage and motivates you to be a team player. It keeps you from cheating on your vows and taking advantage of your partner's vulnerabilities.

**8. TRUST:** How trusting are you, and how trustworthy? This habit helps you believe your partner's motives and actions are true and honest. It provides you with the strength to believe in them and in the partnership. It also motivates you to build trust through your own actions by living up to your promises.

**9. ROMANCE:** Are you romantic? Do you wish for more romance in your marriage? This habit helps you understand what romance is for a man and for a woman. This habit makes your partner feel certain that your love is real and lasting. It shows how to be romantic in ways you have never considered. It stimulates and inspires you to fulfill each other's needs for love and affection.

**10. PERSONAL CARE:** How well do you take care of yourself? Do you know how to care for your own needs so you have the energy to care for others? This habit keeps you motivated to do what you need to keep your mind and body healthy. It shows you how to build self-esteem and strengthen your mental and physical powers so you can meet the challenges of everyday life.

Each of The Ten Habits of Passionate Customer Care is an essential part of an overall network of energy supply that continuously charges and recharges you to care for each other. Practice these habits and you will build the intimacy you need to sustain love over a lifetime. Among the pages ahead you will learn how to develop and exercise all ten of these positive habits.

# 1. ASSESSMENT

The top brass of a Los Angeles radio station told one of their popular program hosts if he wanted to keep people tuned-in, he should talk less and play more music. How did the executives know music was more important to listeners than talk? They learned it from the Arbitron® Portable People Meter, a cell-phone-sized device that a selected group of consumers carry around with them to report their listening habits. Whether they are driving the car or lounging on the beach, the meter tracks their preferences. Nice research tool. Imagine if you could use a customer care meter to gather information to help your relationship. You could make a habit of continually assessing the quality of your marriage.

When management told their talented radio jock to play more music, he wasn't all that happy—until they told him talking less would improve his ratings. He liked the possibility of gaining market share and satisfying listeners, but he would miss being able to express himself on air. After all, what were they paying him for if not his personality? When it comes to marriage, we all like to talk about how we feel, but listening is the best way to assess our partner's needs.

## Evaluating Ourselves Can Be a Shock

Here is an example of how we assessed our ability to manage our consumer products company. When we started our company, we created all the products and ran the company from our home basement. We outsourced manufacturing, fulfillment and sales to other companies. Within three years we grew to a point that it was more practical to open an office and bring in-house everything except manufacturing and product shipping and handling. We hired people in sales, accounting, logistics and design. It was an exciting time. Sales were growing rapidly, and the growth contributed to challenges as we added new faces and responsibilities.

We started regular Monday morning meetings bringing everyone together to coordinate workflow and talk about our growing pains. It soon became obvious that our employees needed another way to speak their minds.

We used a process known as **"STOP-START-CONTINUE"** to help us learn what our employees were thinking. We prepared a questionnaire asking our team three questions:

1) What do you want the company to STOP doing?

2) What do you want the company to START doing?

3) What do you want the company to CONTINUE doing?

The answers came back to us a few days later. We took them home after work that night and began reading, anxious to learn what our team was thinking. Within a few minutes of skimming the results, we stared at each other with disappointed looks.

"What does your first one say?"

"It's not what I expected."

"Mine either."

The more we read, the more depressed we felt. To say we were surprised by the assessments of our management skills would be an understatement. We were devastated. It was hard to read about our shortcomings, especially when we presumed we were doing a good job. Our employees were telling us exactly what we did not expect to hear. In so many words, many felt we were doing a marginal job of running the company.

Sure, we expected to hear a few complaints—ones that could be easily fixed—but we found that half of our employees were unhappy. They wrote that we didn't spend enough time guiding them; they didn't understand what we expected from them; they were afraid to make mistakes, and they didn't have the tools they needed to be effective.

Some felt we weren't giving them enough direction and others felt we were micromanaging. We felt attacked and hurt. How could they be so ungrateful for all we were doing for them? They were well-paid. They had full benefits, liberal vacations and flexible hours. Many of the complaints seemed ridiculous and unfair. The more we read the more upset we got. Before long we were mad enough to fire the whole thoughtless bunch and start over.

After an hour or so of defending our egos—to each other—we settled down and began reflecting on what we had done. We thought we had sent out the questionnaires to uncover a few minor issues that might need tweaking, but we never dreamed *we* could be the problem. We were so angry that we each got up and went off by ourselves and did some things around the house to cool off and get over the shock.

Later we came back together and sat down again to talk. We tried more commiserating, but that didn't accomplish anything. Before long we stopped acting like disgruntled parents and started thinking like marketing people. After all, the whole point of our research was to find out what our employees were thinking and feeling.

Maybe we sent out the questionnaires to get a pat on the back because we thought we were doing so well. That would explain our shock. Maybe we weren't as special as we thought. Still, we weren't naïve enough to believe we didn't have problems.

We are accustomed to market research. When we ask consumers to try one of our new products, we don't anticipate praise. We presume the product has flaws, we just don't know yet what they are. We ask for users' responses to learn what needs improvement.

Over the years we learned how to separate our egos from the product, but evaluating ourselves turned out to be different. In effect, we were asking our employees to judge us. Products don't feel rejected when users trash talk them. Products don't have feelings. People do.

It took a few hours before our temperatures dropped to normal. When the lights came on, the sting faded. We realized we were looking at this evaluation process backward. This wasn't about us. It was about our employees. It was about *their* needs, not ours. We took their responses as personal criticism. It felt like an attack, but in the correct light we realized this wasn't an assessment of us as much as a declaration of what they needed to do their jobs. That's not to say we didn't receive some praise, but it was the problems that needed our attention.

When one employee complained he wanted us to stop micromanaging, he was saying he needed more freedom to make decisions. When another employee wrote that she needed more supervision, she was asking for more guidance in making decisions. Our own needs for approval got in the way of seeing the company from their perspectives. We realized we had to change. We stopped thinking globally and started acting locally. The questionnaire was specific to each person and their personal concerns, so we focused on their individual needs. Now, our job was to sit down with each person and use their assessment to focus on their needs.

## The Relationship Audit

STOP-START-CONTINUE is also a powerful way to talk about your own personal needs in your marriage. This simple assessment method can be applied to virtually every facet of your relationship and the process can become a powerful habit. At first, it may be hard to reveal exactly what you want your partner to STOP or START doing. The CONTINUE part is easier. It's a positive boost, and it's why we leave that question for last. When you ask your partner to assess you, it's vital to avoid hearing their answers as personal criticism. You must frame the answers as declarations of their needs, not your shortcomings.

You must approach this like market researchers looking for ways to make your product more appealing to your customer. For example, in our company, if one of our customers complained about our product or service, we didn't take it as an insult. We worked with them to satisfy their needs. Likewise, by focusing on your partner's needs, not yourself, you will feel less defensive.

> YOU MAY THINK YOU ARE MORE CARING THAN YOUR PARTNER. MAYBE THEY FEEL JUST THE OPPOSITE.

In successful relationships, partners feel the business side of love is pretty balanced. It isn't because they are working the same number of hours each day or week. It's because they feel good about their partner's contribution. The first step in a relationship audit is to select a fertile area for study such as finances. You need to agree about how to manage money, including cash, credit cards, checks and bills. The business side of marriage can be charged with emotion because it threatens independence. It is vital to put yourselves in a market research state of mind—focus on gathering information and not on criticizing each other's spending habits or money management skills.

The audit is not about deciding who is right or wrong about how to handle money. Our STOP-START-CONTINUE questionnaires showed us how our employees felt about the company and their jobs. Asking targeted questions is a great way to find out what you need from each other.

> ### IMAGINING YOUR PARTNER IS A CUSTOMER MAKES IT EASIER TO REMAIN OBJECTIVE AND FEEL LESS DEFENSIVE WHEN YOU DISCOVER THEIR NEEDS.

## Ready, Set, Ask!

To begin your research, pick a subject to discuss such as managing money or doing chores. One of you goes first to ask STOP-START-CONTINUE questions, then it's your partner's turn to ask the questions. The partner asking questions must listen to the answers and not interrupt. After your partner finishes answering, you can ask for clarification. Here is an example of how to use the process. This is a fictional conversation between Sean and Judy about managing money.

JUDY: Is there anything about the way I manage money that you would like me to stop doing?

SEAN: First, I think you are pretty good with money. Okay? I am a little concerned about how many credit cards we have, though, and I'd like to cut the number down to just two.

JUDY: (Interrupting.) We don't have that many cards, Sean.

SEAN: This is supposed to be about finding out what I want you to stop doing. So, first I would like you to stop interrupting. This is about defining our needs, not about defending ourselves. Okay? You asked what I need, and I'm trying to tell you.

JUDY: (Sigh.) You're right. I'm sorry. Go ahead.

SEAN: Anyway, I think we have about six or seven credit cards that we are paying interest on and if we had just two we would consolidate our travel points. It would also seem easier to manage. I carry one card and it seems to work fine.

JUDY: I understand. And I agree. I promise to work on that. Is there anything else you would like me to stop doing when it comes to money?

SEAN: I would like you to stop buying so many shoes and purses. Maybe set a monthly budget just for those two things.

JUDY: I don't buy that many shoes. . . Sorry, okay. I'm not defending myself. I'm just . . . never mind. Go on.

SEAN: That's all I can think of for now.

JUDY: All right. Is there anything you'd like me to start doing?

SEAN: I would like you to start putting money into our savings account each month and pay ourselves before we pay everybody else.

JUDY: Do you have a number in mind?

SEAN: I don't know, maybe five percent of our income.

JUDY: Okay, anything else?

SEAN: Not for now.

JUDY: Is there anything you want me to continue doing?

SEAN: Yes. I want you to continue paying the bills because you're doing a great job. When I did it, I know I was sometimes late writing checks and since you took it over we don't get late notices and our credit score has gone up. I am grateful for all the effort you put in. I do appreciate that you are so well organized. I hope you will continue doing that.

The next step is to reverse the process. Sean asks Judy the same questions.

SEAN: What would you like me to stop doing?

JUDY: I'd like you to stop promising friends that you will loan them money. I have a hard enough time paying bills. I don't want to feel like the bad guy when you tell somebody you will lend them a hundred dollars and then I have to say no or agree with it. I know they won't ever pay it back and probably wouldn't be able to loan us money if we needed it.

SEAN: Judy, I haven't done that since the last time we talked about it, two or three years ago.

JUDY: You're not supposed to object or make excuses. I'm just telling you my feelings.

SEAN: Sorry. I get it. Go ahead. Anything else?

JUDY: I would like you to stop leaving your loose change all over the house. I don't know what to do with it. I don't like picking up pennies and dimes everywhere. I would like you to keep them in one place.

SEAN: Right. I can do that.

JUDY: I wish you would stop forgetting to tell me when you write checks on our account. I find these surprise checks for things I don't know anything about. I can't manage if I don't know what's going on.

SEAN: Okay. I agree that's not good. I understand and I will change.

I promise! Anything else?

JUDY: That's all for now.

SEAN: What do you want me to start doing?

JUDY: I would like you to help me with the budget each month, so we both see how much we are going to spend. That way we can agree so we don't argue over what happened in the past.

SEAN: Okay. What else do you want me to start doing?

JUDY: I want us to work on our retirement program. I like the idea of putting five percent of our income away each month, but we need an IRA or something. Can you start looking into that?

SEAN: Sure I can do that. Anything else? Or can we move on to what you want me to continue doing?

JUDY: I have a few more things, and I can wait on those. I don't want to start sounding like everything is wrong or that I'm not happy, because I am. It's just that I know we have a few kinks that could be worked out. Do you agree?

SEAN: Yes, that's why we're doing this.

JUDY: Okay. Now, the thing I'd like you to continue doing when it comes to money is to keep telling me I am doing an okay job of paying the bills. Sometimes I feel like I'm not doing as much as I should. It just takes a lot of time, and I get overwhelmed when we have something unexpected come up, and I can't pay it right away. So I need to hear you tell me I'm doing a good job.

SEAN: I do. And like I said, I appreciate it.

JUDY: I know this is not exactly about managing money, but I would like you to continue surprising me with flowers when I'm not expecting them. I know you pay for them out of your spending money and it means so much to me. You know I love flowers, but I feel guilty buying them for myself.

SEAN: It's my pleasure.

JUDY: That's all for me . . . for now. So can we go back and talk about the shoes and purses?

SEAN: Absolutely.

## The Dreaded "We Need to Talk"

Even when you know how to use this process, it isn't always easy to get started. One single phrase that raises our defenses is the dreaded, "We need to talk." The partner on the receiving end of this message hears, "You need to listen." Reconciling conflicts in marriage is never easy, but it helps to use a non-threatening approach to get the ball rolling.

In the brick-and-mortar world, stores have a customer care department to take returns and solve customer issues. Let's look at the difference between the "we need to talk" approach and the customer care approach.

If you engaged the person behind a customer counter, you wouldn't say, "We have a problem." You would say, "I have a problem," or, "I need to return this." You wouldn't use the pronoun "we," because the customer service person doesn't have a problem. You have the problem. The customer care representative is there to help you solve it.

> WHEN YOU SAY TO YOUR PARTNER, "WE NEED
> TO TALK," AND THEY DON'T KNOW WHY, IT
> PUTS THEM ON THE DEFENSIVE.

On the other hand, when you say, "I need to talk to you about something," or "I have a problem and I'm hoping you can help me," you are asking for their help instead of implying they've done something wrong. They may be part of the problem but attacking them isn't going to help you solve it.

You are each in charge of customer care for each other. Picture yourself standing behind the customer counter ready to resolve any and all problems your customer might have. American Express trained their customer care people to listen and assess the customer's problems before solving them:

- **Listen** without preconception to understand the problem.

- **Empathize** with your customer's emotional state.

- **Apologize,** regardless of the cause, to reduce defensiveness.

- **Commit** to righting the problem, regardless of what it is.

- **Clarify** the action that will be taken to fix the problem.

- **Ask** your customer if there is anything else they need.

Now, let's do a tongue-in-cheek role play to see how this might work using these steps. Judy is the customer and Sean is behind the customer care counter at retailer Bed, Bath, and Beyond.®

Judy approaches the counter with two wet bath towels in hand.

JUDY: Hi, I'm having a problem with my towels.

SEAN: I'm terribly sorry to hear that. How can I help?

JUDY: As you can see these towels are still wet.

SEAN: Yes, I see that. Why are they wet?

JUDY: Because my husband won't hang them up after he showers.

SEAN: I see, but why are you returning them?

JUDY: Obviously, there is something wrong with them.

SEAN: Why do you think that?

JUDY: If they're too hard for my sweetheart to hang up, they must be defective. There is nothing wrong with him, so it must be the towels.

SEAN: Hmmm. Maybe your husband is just forgetful. Why don't you keep the towels and give him another chance? I'm sure he will come around.

JUDY: You're sure the towels aren't the problem?

SEAN: I'm positive it's not the towels. If he continues to have this problem, you can bring the towels back, and we will gladly refund your money. In the meantime, I will talk to him and make sure he follows through.

JUDY: Thank you so much. You are so helpful.

SEAN: My pleasure. Is there anything else I can help you with, today?

JUDY: Yes, when you talk to my husband please tell him I love him, and if he needs to take a shower in the morning, his towels are in the trunk of my car.

Of course, this is a humorous exaggeration. Few conflicts in life are this easy to resolve, and we don't want to get into the reasons why someone doesn't hang up their wet towels.

The purpose of this role-playing exercise is to show three things: First, how to state the problem using an "I" message. Second, how to listen without being defensive when providing the customer care. Third, it never hurts to add some humor to engage your partner in solving a problem.

## PASSIONATE CUSTOMER CARE MEANS LISTENING OBJECTIVELY AND MAKING CUSTOMERS FEEL VALUED, INSTEAD OF TRYING TO PROVE THEM WRONG.

Acknowledging your customer's right to have their emotions shows acceptance, not rejection. Customer care requires you to listen and not dispute their problem. You need to accept their problem as valid, not minimize it.

The secret to resolving conflict with your partner is remembering your goal. Staying in love is more important than winning any disagreement. To achieve that result, you both must feel and act the same way toward each other at the same time. When you are facing conflict with a partner, you may believe they are wrong about the facts, and they may seem unbearably unreasonable. However, one thing is certain; you both feel you are in the right. To quote Sheriff Ed Tom Bell in Cormac McCarthy's novel, *No Country For Old Men,* "Even the villain is the hero in his own story."

No matter how villainous your partner may seem in a moment of conflict, they too believe they are the hero. Resolving conflict means you both must assess and respect each other's point of view and need each other's understanding and empathy. Recall the Customer Mantra and ask yourself the question: "Right now, how can I treat my partner like my best customer?"

You may not be in the mood to use STOP-START-CONTINUE to talk about a problem. It may feel too formal sometimes. However, once it becomes a habit, couples tell us they use it weekly to start a conversation and stay connected. Some problems don't require the whole process but still require your full attention. You or your partner may need to talk about feelings. If so, say, "I don't need you to do anything, right now. I just need you to listen to what I am feeling."

## TO REALLY LOVE SOMEONE, IT ISN'T NECESSARY TO BELIEVE AS THEY DO. IT IS NECESSARY TO ACCEPT THEIR BELIEFS AS BEING REASONABLE.

## How to Reconcile Love and Conflicting Values

Sure, it can be irritating when your partner leaves wet towels on the floor. You could hang their towels and easily solve the problem, or you could remind them to do it. But more serious problems, the kind that tests our deeply held beliefs, are usually filled with more emotion. Serious conflicts involve opposing values and embedded points of view. If you like chick flicks and your partner likes action movies it doesn't matter much, but if you are a Jew and your partner is a Muslim, you either accept each other's values or you won't make it together.

## HOW FAR CAN YOUR VALUES STRETCH AND NOT PULL YOUR MARRIAGE APART AT THE SEAMS?

How much would each of us be willing to modify our individual values in the name of love? At the heart of conflict resolution is the willingness to meet our partners somewhere between opposing ends of what we call The Value Spectrum.

Negotiating a business deal can be pleasurable or perilous depending on how the parties' interests are aligned. When one side needs to make the deal more than the other, or one side has more leverage, or their goals are in opposition, the imbalance often sets up a top dog-underdog dynamic that can breed resentment and deceit. This is a recipe for disaster. Most conflicts fall somewhere along The Value Spectrum line. Earlier in this chapter, we examined Judy's and Sean's competing values regarding shoes and purses. Let's see how The Value Spectrum can help them clarify their differences.

## THE VALUE SPECTRUM

Save _____ Spend

Sean                                    Judy

### Shoes and Purses

Pick a point along the Save__ Spend line. The farther apart you are, the more you need to get into your partner's head and try to empathize with their spot on the scale. It's difficult for a man to empathize with a woman's value for accessories such as shoes, purses and jewelry, just as she may not grasp his need for woodworking tools or skeet-shooting supplies. The conflict arises when they need to divide limited resources.

For Judy and Sean, the question is how much to save for distant retirement vs. how to satisfy immediate desires. Talking about their mutual goals and feelings will help them find ways to accommodate both their desires. When you plot your desires along The Value Spectrum, you can choose any issue and see how your feelings compare.

## CUSTOMER SATISFACTION IS ABOUT PLEASING THE CUSTOMER, NOT YOURSELF.

The beauty of doing your best for the customer is knowing that when they are delighted, you will be too. When you imagine yourselves as customers of each other, each trying to please the other, you move from opposite ends of The Value Spectrum toward meeting at the center. When you see through your partner's eyes and feel through their emotions, it's easier to give up something, (saving or spending) to get something (partner's satisfaction). In the case of shoes and purses, Judy must decide that in order to satisfy Sean's need she has to pull back on her own, and he does the same recognizing that fashion is a currency for Judy. Having no new shoes and purses would deprive her of something she deeply values.

## IT'S EASIER TO FEEL EMPATHY WHEN YOU KNOW WHY A CUSTOMER FEELS CERTAIN NEEDS. STILL, IT'S ESSENTIAL TO RESPECT YOUR CUSTOMER'S NEED REGARDLESS OF THEIR REASON.

Finding your mutual comfort zone on The Value Spectrum is the challenge you face living together. You can give a little to get a little, as in compromise, or you can work together to find a creative alternative. Sean's problem may not be *how many* shoes and purses Judy buys. He may be worried about the total amount of money she spends. A solution could be to agree on the total dollars each can spend, and if she can find a cheaper source of supply, she can buy as many accessories as she desires.

The answer to resolving competing customer needs lies in discovering where each partner's values fit on the spectrum and finding a solution that moves both partners closer to the center. Some values are harder to reconcile. Take their religious convictions, for example. Sean is a Catholic and Judy is a Jew. They have to decide about how they will raise their children. Assuming they are willing to continue to treat each other as customers, would they be able to satisfy each other's needs, especially if they are influenced by extended family values? They may have parents or brothers and sisters who are pressuring them to continue worshiping along family lines. This, as the saying goes, puts them between a "rock and a hard place." They must reconcile their individual needs with their family needs.

### THE VALUE SPECTRUM

Catholicism _____Judaism

               Sean                        Judy

Religion for the Kids

Sean and Judy are on opposite ends of The Value Spectrum. If they refuse to budge, it might be too much to overcome. If they each recognize the importance of their partner's values, they might even try to raise the kids in both, alternating weeks or services and important rituals. Staying in love is about working together to find ways to satisfy your partner's needs, often at the expense of your own. The Value Spectrum will help you understand exactly where your partner stands on any specific ideal, or issue. From there you can work together to mold a solution to satisfy each other.

## Reconciling High-Tech Conflict

In the early days of television, channels and programs were limited. The family crowded around a single set to watch the popular shows of the week. It was a communal event. The news was controlled by three national networks and a few news agencies. High technology changed everything. The more we rely on computers, smart phones, email, texting, gaming and social networks, the more individualized families' tastes have become. The smart tablet, the smart phone, instant messaging and streaming media make it possible for everyone in the family to entertain or inform themselves in different ways at the same time. This creates an opportunity for increased communication and engagement but also delivers constant interruption and something called "social media addiction."

"The jury is still out on whether social media can truly feed an addiction," writes author Carianne King at SocialMediaToday.com. "In the meantime, it's become a daily habit for many, and for some, a lion's share of the day's attention. "

Research shows that 28 percent of iPhone users check their social media channels before getting out of bed in the morning. Teenagers aged 15 to 19 spend at least three hours a day looking at their social channels, and 18 percent of social media users say they can't go more than a few hours without checking out what's happening on social. Whether you are heavy or light users of gadgets, games, media and communication, the more attention you give to your tools, the less time you have to care for each other. This gives rise to conflicts that are hard to resolve unless you give it a serious discussion.

THE VALUE SPECTRUM

Light _____ Heavy

Gadget or Social Media User

When it comes to social media use, it's not easy to measure how much time you spend. You can learn more about your true love's needs and expectations by using STOP-START-CONTINUE and The Value Spectrum to clarify and compare each other's feelings about technology and social media. Nothing can prevent you from becoming more observant, more thoughtful and more curious about your partner's needs. Reconciling conflict will get you closer to showing your true love that you care about their needs and are committed to acting in ways that show how much you want to stay in love.

## How to Assess Your Partner's Needs

How good are you at assessing your partner's needs? In business, we call it market research. Unless you ask for feedback from your customer, you won't know how to give them passionate care. Quit guessing and start asking. It's like the survey we conducted to find out what our employees needed from us to succeed at their jobs. It wasn't easy to be reminded that we aren't perfect, but as painful as it felt in the beginning, what we learned helped us build a stronger company. Likewise, you can build a stronger relationship by satisfying each other's needs. First, you must discover what those needs are. "Nothing can be changed until it is faced," wrote James Baldwin.

## Habit Self-Assessment

At the end of each chapter, you'll find a series of five statements designed for you to assess the level of customer care you give your partner and to help you develop a habit of thinking about your everyday actions. The purpose of these questions is to make you think about your own behavior, not your partner's.

Each of you can use a separate sheet of paper to record your assessments. Then come together and share your results. A rating of "nine" means you "agree" with the statement. A "one" rating means you "disagree." Use your answers to start a conversation about your perceptions and expectations. Perhaps you've never thought about the level of care you give your partner. You feel you just do what needs to be done. The questions may take time to think through. Statement number one, for example, reads: "I show respect for my partner's opinions." Before rating, think of some concrete examples that support your rating. What have you done, in the past and lately, to respect their opinions? When you finish and feel ready to share each other's evaluations, use the STOP-START-CONTINUE process to decide what to do about what you discover. Remember this is about giving your partner the kind of customer care they need.

Aristotle said, "We are what we repeatedly do." Experts say it takes at least 21 days of practice to create a new habit. It's important to give one another time to adjust to creating new habits and stopping objectionable ones. As partners, you must have each other's backs and agree to be patient and tolerant as you forge your caring relationship. Talk about one another's needs with the goal of bringing you closer. Also be aware that this process could open old wounds if you don't trust each other. Keep the mission in mind—to stay in love. Understanding each other's needs brings greater intimacy and increases the possibility of making your marriage all you hoped it would be.

A good sense of humor also helps you reduce tensions as you work ideas out. Do your best not to feel attacked when your partner is talking. If you are faced with a lot of behaviors your partner wants you to change, agree to the one you'll commit to working on first.

## Habit Focus 1. ASSESSMENT

1. I show respect for my partner's opinions.

| 1 | 2 | 3 | 4 | 5 | 6 | 7 | 8 | 9 |

2. I make my partner feel valued.

| 1 | 2 | 3 | 4 | 5 | 6 | 7 | 8 | 9 |

3. I show I'm willing to compromise.

| 1 | 2 | 3 | 4 | 5 | 6 | 7 | 8 | 9 |

4. I accept criticism from my partner.

| 1 | 2 | 3 | 4 | 5 | 6 | 7 | 8 | 9 |

5. I don't try to change my partner.

| 1 | 2 | 3 | 4 | 5 | 6 | 7 | 8 | 9 |

# 2. Preparation

In 2008 Mary Lou's dad died from the aftereffects of a fall. Bob was 90 years old. Shortly after Bob's passing, Mary Lou's mother, Mary Ann, became ill and had to have a series of surgeries leaving her confined to a wheelchair for a long time. Mary Ann is now 96 and going strong with the aid of a walker she calls "Johnny." She is a sweet, charming woman who needs 24/7 care. She can't do most of the simple things we take for granted such as opening the refrigerator or making herself a cup of coffee.

*Dennis:* Confession time. I wasn't prepared to care full-time for a parent. But, you know what? Not being prepared to care for Mary Ann taught me something about how to care. Here's a small example. Mary Lou and I don't usually drink coffee after a meal, but Mary Ann likes to enjoy a cup. We have a single-cup coffee maker so it's easy to make a cup just for her. Here is the rub. We might brew Mary

Ann a cup and place it on the table. Does she drink it? No. She gets distracted watching birds or rabbits outside our window and forgets to drink. She is famous for wanting her coffee extremely hot, so hot that it would burn anyone else's mouth. After fifteen minutes or so, when her coffee cools and she hasn't touched it, she will take a sip and frown. She doesn't say anything, but she also doesn't drink the coffee.

I used to get mildly irritated by this routine. But I couldn't bear to watch her sit there looking down into her cup and not drinking, so I would ask her if she wanted me to heat her coffee. She would brighten up and look very appreciative while apologizing for causing a problem. We would assure her that it was no problem, and Mary Lou or I would stick the cup in the microwave and reheat the coffee. However, that also reheated the ceramic cup making it almost too hot to touch. To solve that problem, we poured the hot coffee into an empty cup. This ritual might repeat itself one or more times at each sitting.

Mary Lou didn't feel this was a problem, but she is a more naturally caring person than me. In the beginning, however, this coffee ceremony got under my skin. I started wondering why I felt imposed upon? Am I just a selfish toad? Would I treat Mary Lou the same way if she were incapable of caring for herself?

## I EVENTUALLY REALIZED THAT I WASN'T LOOKING FOR WAYS TO CARE, I WAS LOOKING FOR WAYS TO AVOID.

I was acting like the guy who suddenly needs to use the bathroom when it's time to wash Thanksgiving dishes. I have always been ready to take care of myself, but I realized I was not prepared to care for Mary Ann. From this, I learned that by developing a habit of preparing myself to reheat her coffee, I could also prepare myself to care when it came time to attend to her other needs. This epiphany made it easier for me to prepare for a lot of other caring behavior.

## THE PROBLEM WITH CARING IS FEELING IT, BUT NOT SHOWING IT.

At some level, we all think we are caring people, perhaps even heroic. Yet, somehow we don't always get around to demonstrating even minor, much less heroic, deeds for the people who need to be cared for. The opportunities to show we care are everywhere, but we often miss them because we are focused on our own needs.

Demands on our time, things that get in the way of our personal plans, and stuff that saps our energy all stand in the way of caring. Ironically, the very times we feel irritated or frustrated with our partners are the best times to demonstrate care. If you are prepared to care, when minor aggravations arise in your relationship, you can turn resentment or apathy into positive action and customer satisfaction.

## Prepare to Be Inconvenienced

*Dennis:* One day Mary Lou and I got in the car to run some errands. A few miles from home she realized she forgot her cell phone. We have all done this, yet for some twisted reason when I'm driving I feel resistance to turn back, as if taking five extra minutes to reverse direction is retreating from a Manifest Destiny. As the driver, I had a choice. I could complain that we didn't have time to go back, though in this particular case we had the whole afternoon to do whatever we wanted. In the past, I might have resisted turning the car around, but this time I didn't complain. I heard a version of the Customer Mantra ringing in my head: *"Right now, what if Mary Lou were my best customer?"* Without saying a word, I made a quick U-turn at the next intersection and headed for home. That single thought—how would she want to be treated—helped me give her the care she needed.

## THE MOMENT YOU FEEL INCONVENIENCED BY YOUR PARTNER IS THE PERFECT OPPORTUNITY TO SHOW THEM HOW MUCH YOU CARE.

You can grouse and complain when your partner asks you to do something they can't accomplish at the moment. Or you can use that moment to be a hero. Maybe they're tied up in traffic and can't pick up the kids from school or soccer practice. Perhaps they need to shop for a present at the last minute because they forgot a birthday. These are moments made for caring. They are chances to step in and ask an essential customer care question, "How can I help you?"

**Dennis:** Occasionally, I forget to set the garbage out to be collected early the next morning. I'm already in bed curling up with a Lee Child novel when I hear the faint rumble of the garage door rising, and I know Mary Lou is putting the garbage cans out on the street. It's my job, but tonight she knows I forgot. She's still up and dressed, so she takes care of the job for me. And the beauty is, when she comes back into the bedroom she never says a word about the favor she has done.

I used to feel guilty about shirking a duty. I even pretended not to notice her support so I wouldn't have to admit my lapse of responsibility. This may seem like a minor issue, but it is worth noting for a couple of reasons. When I didn't acknowledge her favor, I wasn't prepared to care, so I missed a chance to make her feel appreciated. Pretending not to acknowledge her actions made me feel like a troll, and I'd get angry with myself. My sullen mood would make her wonder if I was mad at her for something. Fortunately, somewhere along the way, Mary Lou taught me that a simple "thank you" is a welcome form of reciprocal care. Now, when she does things for me that might have slipped my mind, I thank her with gusto knowing that I will have a chance to reciprocate by doing something for her such as the grocery shopping while she is engrossed in a knitting project.

*Mary Lou:* Because we work and live together, our personal and business conversations and tasks overlap. I like to plan ahead and start each day with a to-do list that includes personal and business goals. It's easy to feel irritated when Dennis asks me to stop what I am doing to focus on something he needs that isn't on my list. The choice to care or complain is mine, but when I am prepared for interruptions, I can welcome them as opportunities to show how much I care. In those moments, we both feel better about ourselves and our partnership.

---

*Develop Your Preparation Habit:*

*Today, prepare yourself to feel inconvenienced. Wait for your partner to do something that's irritated you in the past. Instead of grousing, do something to surprise and delight rather than complain and slight.*

---

## Prepare for Adventure

*Dennis:* Mary Lou likes adventure. One day she asked me if I would like to see a meteor shower. Knowing her keen interest in weather and astronomy, I thought she might be referring to a program on the Discovery Channel. It turned out to be more than that.

Witnessing a true meteor shower was high on the list of things she wanted to see in her lifetime. So when she read that our Southern California desert sky was about to be treated with a full-fledged torrent of shooting stars, she got excited and said she wanted me to watch with her. I made a wild guess that this event would take place at night. She explained that the best viewing time was between 2:00 AM and 4:00 AM. When I heard that, I admit to pausing before asking her if we could see it from our backyard. No, we could not, but we were in luck because astronomers announced one of the best viewing spots in the country was Joshua Tree National Park, about an hour from our home in La Quinta, California. I was a little worried about staying up all night. We had sold our business a few years earlier, but my current hobby/obsession was trading stocks, and the market opened at 6:30 AM on the West Coast. If we stayed up until 4:00 AM watching meteors, I was worried that I wouldn't be alert the rest of the day. I didn't mention my concern to Mary Lou, though, because I was afraid she would either drop the idea of her meteor hunt, or she would go alone and I would miss sharing the experience with her. So, I said I would love to join her.

*Mary Lou:* I was glad Dennis came with me because I didn't want to go alone on the highway and into a park at 2:00 AM. I didn't share that with him when I asked him to go, so it meant a lot that he wanted to be with me. I knew it would impinge on his stock trading and it meant so much to me that he put my wishes first.

*Dennis:* We left home a little after midnight under a clear August sky and a typical 98 degrees. An hour from home we exited the freeway and drove north on a gravel road, eventually pulling into a little campground where a half-dozen other cars were already parked anticipating the show. We angled the car to face northwest because that was supposed to be the ideal viewing direction. A full moon provided enough light for us to get out of the car and spread a pair of beach towels on the hood. We scooted our bodies up onto the warm car and rested the backs of our heads on the windshield so we could gaze comfortably up at the night sky. Astronomers predicted that the meteors would light up the sky at the rate of one per minute, so we were anticipating quite a show.

It turns out, however, that meteors do not run on schedules or appear at any particular rate; nor did this event resemble anything close to a shower. Over the next few hours, lying side by side, we observed no more than a dozen streaks of light, each lasting merely seconds. Mary Lou was supremely disappointed, and I for her. But stretched out on the hood of our car, awash in moonlight, we enjoyed another kind of reward.

We were together with no distractions. It felt like we had all of the time in the world to stare at the heavens and marvel at the vastness of the universe, and to share our latest thoughts about the meaning of life. And she got to relive, one more time, my reminiscence of the moment I first set eyes on her. It's amazing how, after so many years of marriage, we can still be in love, not a little, but a lot.

Hunting meteors is a little like chasing rainbows which we have also done many times during our marriage. Lying out there in the middle of the desert, in deep night, was one of those moments that we will always remember. These are the moments that help us stay in love. Spontaneity is the spice in a caring relationship.

We all have those times in our lives when our partners want us to do something that doesn't excite us. Overcoming selfish inertia, getting off our butts to do things for each other, is not necessarily built into the human psyche. A business, too, can grow stale through complacency. We need an incentive to pull us out of our comfort zones. We need something to remind us that life is not always about me.

## ADVENTURES DON'T HAVE TO BE EXPENSIVE OR ELABORATE, THEY JUST HAVE TO BE OUTSIDE OF THE ROUTINE.

Whenever Mary Lou asks me to do something that doesn't necessarily excite me, I imagine she's my customer, one who means so much to me that my company would go bankrupt without her. Then I imagine that by fulfilling her needs, I will land the biggest, most profitable purchase order of my life.

I know that if customers asked me to join them in watching a meteor shower I would jump at the chance. It would be an ideal opportunity to build the relationship and help to assure future business. So why shouldn't I show the same enthusiasm when my wife asks me to do something that I may not be excited about?

Mary Lou is more important than any customer I will ever have, and yet thinking of her as a customer helps me step away from our relationship and feel her needs with a different urgency. It's a trick of the mind, especially for business people who can easily relate.

By thinking of each other as indispensable customers, we take them out of the familiar and see a different view of their importance and value. The Customer Mantra is a useful reminder that satisfying our partners assures a profitable future together.

---

*Develop Your Preparation Habit:*

*Today, prepare yourself for adventure. Do something your partner has talked about wanting to do, but you avoided in the past because it didn't interest you. Show that you want to add something new to your relationship by focusing on their needs.*

---

## Prepare for the Unexpected

*Mary Lou:* Two weeks after the infamous 9/11/2001 attacks on the World Trade Center, our son Dennis Jr. was getting married in Black Butte, Oregon. Black Butte is an idyllic vacation spot where our beautiful daughter-in-law, Kathleen, had spent her summers growing up. Coordinating our travels to the wedding was a challenge. Dennis Jr. and Kathleen both lived in Seattle, Washington. Kathleen's parents, Bud and Helen Hanzel, lived in Salem, Oregon. We lived outside of

Denver, Colorado. My parents, Bob and Mary Ann Wickens, lived in Albuquerque, New Mexico. Literally, all of the family and most of the guests were from somewhere other than where the wedding was to take place. That meant traveling at a precarious time. Luckily we had made all of our reservations well in advance.

My folks were scheduled to fly to Denver to meet us so we could all fly together to Portland, Oregon and then by small plane to Bend, Oregon. We had arranged for a wheelchair to shuttle my mom from her flight to the connecting flight almost a quarter of a mile down the Denver International Airport concourse. We arrived at the new gate just as the flight to Portland was loading.

Minutes later my mom and dad settled into seats behind the bulkhead. Mom asked me for her small black carry-on case that held her toiletries and medicines. I didn't recall seeing it, nor did Dennis or Dad. Then she remembered that she had tucked it in the overhead bin on the previous flight and forgot to retrieve it when she got off. The flight attendants were about to close the doors and prepare for take-off. Mom couldn't leave without her medicines. I rushed up to an attendant and explained the problem. She instantly grasped the urgency and told another attendant to hold the door open. She turned to us and said, "No bag left behind," and rushed off the plane and up the boarding ramp.

We all guessed she would call someone at the other gate to search for the bag. What if the cleaning crew had already finished going through the other plane and taken the carry-on to Lost and Found? How would we ever find it? Should we get off the plane and make sure we secured the medicine case? If we did, we might not be able to reschedule another flight in time to make the wedding. The other attendants assured Mom they wouldn't take off without her medicine—if they could find it. We waited five minutes, then ten minutes. Passengers all around us were becoming restless and wanted to know what was going on. Why weren't we taking off? Word spread that something was wrong. Was the flight being delayed? Was someone sick or injured?

Suddenly, the flight attendant reappeared out of breath and clutching the black overnight case as if it were the Holy Grail. She held it high for us to see. "Is this it?" she asked with a broad smile. My mom reached out for the case as nearby passengers clapped in appreciation. It turned out the attendant raced up and back from one plane to the other to recover the bag for a woman she had never met and would likely never see again. Why? She wasn't just doing her job. She was proving the power of passionate care. She said it was a pleasure to serve us, and it is my pleasure to retell the story.

We will never forget Frontier Airlines Flight Attendant Mary—yes, that was her name—because of her thoughtfulness. She'll always symbolize care. Doing the unexpected for our spouses can have the same impact on our personal relationships as the ones we experience in our public contacts. Whenever we go out of our way to show special care, we can be assured of being remembered. The Customer Mantra reminds us to be on the lookout for unexpected opportunities to care. Like Mary, we never know when an occasion will present itself for us to go out of our way to become heroes—especially for the ones we love.

## CARING FOR OTHERS DOESN'T HAVE TO BE SHOWY OR GRAND. THE SIMPLEST GENEROSITIES PROVE THAT WE CARE.

Showing your true love they matter, every day, in special ways, will ensure that you get what every business owner dreams of—gaining a happy customer for life. Examples of great customer care are all around us. And if passionate care works to build customer loyalty in business, think about what it could do for a marriage. Our challenge is to adapt customer caring methods wherever we find them and turn them into rewards for each other, not just on birthdays and anniversaries, but every day. We can also turn chores into gifts that will make us feel rewarded.

---

*Develop Your Preparation Habit:*

*Today, be on the lookout for something unexpected. It can be a problem your partner never saw coming, such as a dead battery, a lost cell phone or a frozen computer. Be ready to help and support them any way you can.*

---

## Prepare by Modeling

We can borrow from our everyday business encounters and adapt and apply the care we receive to our personal relationships. Waitpersons who provide superior service receive more generous tips, not merely for their efficiency but for how well we feel they have served us. If they fill our water glass without being asked, we feel their care even if we didn't notice it until we needed a drink.

When they spot that we need an extra napkin or a clean fork to replace the one we dropped on the floor, we appreciate they're looking out for us. When they take our order right away, because we are in a hurry, and they keep us informed of the kitchen's progress, we sense they care.

We reward these and other caring actions even though they may lie outside of our conscious awareness. One study showed that waitresses improved their tips merely by being more personal. Customers rewarded them for smiling more often and for caring gestures such as lightly touching the customer's shoulder or the back of their hand while taking an order.

## DOING WHATEVER YOU CAN TO SHOW YOU CARE CAN PREVENT ROUTINE FROM NUMBING YOU DOWN.

At home, it should be just as easy to be warm and welcoming, to brush each other on the arm or back, to kiss each other lightly in passing, and never leave the house without whispering a word of affection. You don't have to leave a tip under your plate, but whoever makes dinner or does the dishes deserves a kiss on the cheek, a hug, or some other outward show of appreciation.

*Develop Your Preparation Habit:*

*Today, heighten your awareness of the world around you and seek to model caring behavior that you observe in others. If you see someone go out of their way to help someone, or you hear a co-worker praise someone for a job well done, find a way to emulate their behavior with your partner.*

## Prepare for Fresh Ways to Care

Some psychologists suggest it helps to think back to the things we did for each other when we first began dating. Often, this advice is about reconstructing familiar romantic settings such as dining under candlelight or spur-of-the-moment romantic getaways. These actions certainly demonstrate love and are a part of what we call passionate care. But the truth is we can never fully duplicate the pleasure we felt in the formative years of our relationship. Well into a marriage, life has changed. We have changed. The rock concert, rave or picnic in the park we lived for when dating no longer provide the same thrill. Those first experiences have become fond memories, not heart-thumping, fist-pumping confirmations of our burning love. As we age and change, we need to find new opportunities, new ways of caring for each other that fit who we are at this stage in our relationship.

## PAY ATTENTION TO WHAT'S INSIDE YOUR PARTNER'S MIND AND HEART AND WHO THEY ARE TODAY.

For a woman, romance may be found in flowers, or jewelry, or a poem written only for them, but passionate care might also mean taking out the garbage without needing to be reminded. Caring may be about changing the baby's diapers because you want to or voicing approval for what a great job she's done decorating the house. A bed with turned-down sheets and a chocolate on the pillow like they offer in better hotels could mean the world. Maybe she would like a compliment for how she handled a difficult situation with the kids, an achievement in her job, or seriously, her new shoes.

For a man, passionate care may mean a week with no honey-do chores. It may mean praise for his integrity, his intelligence and hard work. It could be time for himself or a word of appreciation for how he pays the bills on time. It may mean preparing a special meal that he loves but hasn't tasted in a while. Passionate care is about finding out what makes our mates feel loved—now—and delivering the goods.

*Develop Your Preparation Habit:*

*Today, add something new to your routine. If you each do the same chores throughout the week, trade one or two of them to gain empathy for each other's work. It will help you understand what problems they are solving that you take for granted.*

## Prepare to Engage

A study at the University of North Carolina found that touching, holding hands and hugging releases oxytocin, called the "bonding" hormone, into the bloodstream causing feelings of elation and affection. (Oxytocin is not to be confused with the prescription painkiller Oxycodone.) A considerable body of research over many years has shown that oxytocin also promotes greater sexual receptivity by increasing the production of testosterone, which influences sex drive in both men and women.

### ONE OF THE EASIEST AND MOST SATISFYING WAYS TO CARE FOR EACH OTHER IS THE 20-SECOND HUG.

On average, the adult male body produces up to ten times more testosterone than the female, but from a behavioral perspective, females are more sensitive to this hormone.

Every hug, especially one lasting 20 seconds, helps us stay in love by releasing oxytocin, thereby increasing the desire for sex, which further increases the production of oxytocin, creating a virtuous cycle of affection.

---

*Develop Your Preparation Habit:*

*Today, before you leave for work, or when you come home, hold each other for a full 20 seconds. The first time you do this, count to 20 together out loud so you get a feel for how long 20 seconds really lasts. You may become anxious and want to break away at first, but hold on. In time it can feel as essential as your morning coffee or tea.*

## Prepare for Appreciation

Unexpected and spontaneous engagement offers additional bonuses. This may sound contradictory, but it is possible to plan for spontaneity. For example, we might feel like praising our sweethearts for something they have accomplished. If we are prepared because we've purchased congratulatory cards in advance, we are ready when the moment arises. We usually assume that we will get a present from our partners on our birthdays, but what about a card or cake on days they don't expect them, just to say we are glad they were born? We can do these things if we are prepared to care.

A flower for no special reason is a delight and easy to do if you know where the flower shops are located. A pack of golf balls, or any little out-of-the-ordinary gift can pick up your favorite customer's day and is easy to accomplish if you've already bought them before they're needed. You can tell yourself that you care because you feel deep emotion, but the only way your partner feels proof of your love is when you show it, not once in a while, but every day. To believe that your partner should know how you feel and doesn't need to be reminded of your love is a mistake of arrogance. It's like buying groceries at the supermarket every week and never hearing that your patronage is appreciated. Are you supposed to assume management loves you? It's still important to hear it.

*Develop Your Preparation Habit:*

*Today, stop at the market and buy three thank-you cards and keep them in your desk, at the office or at home. Keep them ready to thank your partner for something you don't normally thank them for. They will feel great and so will you.*

## Prepare a Foundation of Care to Build On

*Mary Lou:* After my dad, Robert Wickens, married my mom Mary Ann Franey, he brought her a single red rose on their first month anniversary. The second month he gave her two roses. Month three he came with three roses and so on until the twelfth month when he presented her with a dozen red roses to celebrate their first year together. The first month his gift was unexpected. The second month two roses were a delightful surprise. The third month, and for each successive month, my mother learned to expect roses. But the growing anticipation she felt as each month approached outweighed the element of surprise. Bob's roses were an ever-increasing proof of his love and the foundation for a marriage that lasted sixty years.

---

*Develop Your Preparation Habit:*

*Start a new tradition you will both look forward to doing once a week or month. Set it on your calendar until it becomes second nature. Make sure it is for just the two of you. Maybe it's as simple as getting a hot dog together for lunch at Costco, working out together, going to a movie or getting a yogurt. Make it something you look forward to sharing on a regular basis.*

---

Never pass up an opportunity to prepare for love. Establishing a pattern of caring behavior gets you going in the right direction. You've heard the saying, "You never get a second chance to make a first impression." While that is true, don't overlook another truth.

### YOU CAN NEVER DAZZLE YOUR FAVORITE CUSTOMER TOO SOON.

Every time you go out of your way to demonstrate love, you build a little more of the house that rests on the foundation you set at the beginning of your relationship. Solid foundations are essential for good beginnings, and you need to keep building on them to prepare for what is ahead. To succeed in business you can never give up looking for opportunities to dazzle your favorite customer. To succeed in marriage you must do even more. You must prepare your imagination to look for new ways to delight the real VIP of your life, your "Very Important Partner." How well are you prepared to care? Below are five Habit Focus questions for this chapter to help you develop your Habit of Preparation. The purpose of these questions is to make you think about your own level of care, not your partner's care. Remember this is about giving your partner the kind of customer care they need.

## Habit Focus 2. PREPARATION

1. I often help my partner without being asked.

| 1 | 2 | 3 | 4 | 5 | 6 | 7 | 8 | 9 |

2. I often praise my partner for little things.

| 1 | 2 | 3 | 4 | 5 | 6 | 7 | 8 | 9 |

3. I spontaneously surprise my partner.

| 1 | 2 | 3 | 4 | 5 | 6 | 7 | 8 | 9 |

4. I tell my partner they are appreciated.

| 1 | 2 | 3 | 4 | 5 | 6 | 7 | 8 | 9 |

5. I hug my partner every day.

| 1 | 2 | 3 | 4 | 5 | 6 | 7 | 8 | 9 |

# 3. RESPECT

Experts say that marriage requires compromise. Still, it's not easy for strong-willed couples to temper their needs in favor of each other. We learned early in our relationship that if we were going to make it together as a couple, and moreover as entrepreneurs, we needed to respect each other's ideas, judgments and points of view and still maintain our individual identities.

The following nine types of respect reveal the many different ways we can reward each other by recognizing and honoring one another's unique qualities.

## Respect Each Other's Interests

For the purposes of this book, the word "interests" carries two different meanings. The first is *personal interests* such as hobbies, pastimes, entertainment and intellectual pursuits. The second is *aligned interests* such as shared goals and objectives. To help us see how aligned interests can change, let's consider a young married couple named

Sarah and Kristen. In the beginning of their marriage, they shared a love of camping, hiking and biking. Kristen is a lawyer and Sarah is an event planner. Together they enjoyed touring the back roads of the neighboring countryside. They camped out and rock climbed as if they were training for competition. Their *aligned interest* in the outdoors and their mutual competitiveness filled their weekends and vacations.

Then life began to change.

As their careers blossomed and their job responsibilities grew, they found less time to share their favorite pastime. Kristen was trying to make partner in her law firm so she increased her billable hours and worked more weekends. At the same time, Sarah's company expanded to a national scale, taking her away to distant events.

Sarah loved the travel, but it kept her away from home as much as two weekends a month. With less time for their shared pursuits of biking and hiking, Kristen took up tennis. Sarah started out with her, but then tore her ankle ligaments stepping off a curb at a corporate event in Chicago.

While Sarah was sidelined for two months, Kristen moved up the tennis ladder to ever stiffer competition. Sarah was unable to play but also realized she didn't enjoy tennis. She mentioned that to a friend who introduced her to bridge. She discovered she did enjoy it, but Kristen didn't.

It wasn't long before Kristen was spending her weekends competing in tennis tournaments while Sarah immersed herself in bridge tournaments. Their aligned interest in the outdoors faded and was replaced by personal interests, which served as fodder for arguments. It wasn't long before they blamed each other for being unwilling to give up their "thing" to open more time for doing things together. This is how couples' common interests become diverted by time, changes in job, health or other forces. The challenge of marriage is respecting each other's individual pursuits and at the same time aligning your interests so you don't grow apart.

## ALIGNED INTERESTS IS A BUSINESS CONCEPT, EQUALLY RELEVANT IN MARRIAGE.

In a business, investors, founders, managers and employees all must align their interests and goals in order to succeed and grow. Unaligned interests cause problems. Investors want to build sales fast and sell the company to recoup their investment, but the company founder may want to maintain control and create a legacy to pass on to children and grandchildren.

At the same time, key managers may hope to take over the company in a leveraged buyout, and employees want to work for a growing company that offers long-term jobs with good chances for advancement.

Finding common purpose is difficult if not impossible when there are too many competing interests. Conflict may be inevitable, yet not necessarily apparent until each party feels the friction from not getting their own way. The same is true in marriage if interests, pastimes, goals and objectives are misaligned. The goal is finding a way to respect each other's needs.

It's easier to appreciate our partners' eccentricities when we think of them as customers. We wouldn't tell a customer, or even imply, that their favorite pastime or hobby was silly or a dreary waste. If a customer invited us to a bridge or a tennis tournament, we would be delighted for the chance to build the relationship even if bridge or tennis bored us to tears. When customers extend an invitation to join them at some event, we jump at the chance, maybe because we like the customer or can visualize a reward. Showing interest in the customer's life gives us a better chance for continued business.

When Kristen invites Sarah to a tennis match, Sarah may be more likely to want to go if she can imagine a reward, such as Kristen attending one of her bridge events. When they biked and hiked together they were rewarding each other through sharing something they both loved. As their individual needs changed, they needed new ways to show they still cared about each other.

Respecting each other's interests is a powerful form of caring. Doing something we don't enjoy may seem like a sacrifice, but when we think of it as a relationship-builder with our favorite customer, it is easier to stay true to the mission of staying in love.

## WHEN YOU SHOW RESPECT FOR YOUR PARTNER'S HOBBIES AND PURSUITS, YOU BUILD A BRIDGE TO ALIGN YOUR LARGER GOALS.

Just as business stakeholders prosper when goals are aligned, so do couples. Showing interest in each other's pastimes makes it easier to align long-term interests. It's easier to respect a partner's desire for starting a business, changing jobs, having children, going back to school, or making any major life decision if we respect each other's everyday interests.

Respect sets a tone of cooperation that's vital in the face of high stress or tragedy that tests the strength of our marriages. Owning a company together, as we did, required an even higher level of aligned interests. Our company's mission was *to create and market simple consumer products that solved everyday problems in unique and entertaining ways.* It was a risky enterprise fraught with fast-paced decisions.

## WHEN OPERATING A BUSINESS TOGETHER, YOU COULD EASILY RESENT EACH OTHER UNLESS YOU SHARE AN OCEAN OF RESPECT FOR ONE ANOTHER'S INTERESTS.

Together we gave birth to more than 50 simple consumer products. In order to succeed, we had to see the same big picture and agree on a way to frame it. That's virtually impossible if you don't respect and value each other's point of view.

It's one thing to agree on the budget for business expenses, or for manufacturing a product, but what happens when one partner thinks they have a great idea and the other thinks it's a "dog with fleas?" It can be hard to agree on product names, market position, packaging, color, size, shape or retail price.

The most important quality partners can have is a kind of "humble arrogance." You have to confidently express your beliefs and interests knowing your ideas alone are not enough for a complete solution to any problem. Why? In marriage, as in business, every problem encompasses both of you, so the solution has to satisfy your mutual as well as individual interests.

## IT TAKES THOUGHTFUL CARE TO APPRECIATE EACH OTHER'S INTERESTS.

Over time, we developed a process for creating our products and along the way we discovered that problems related to the business side of marriage, those everyday details that require constant care, were similar to what we faced when creating new products. To align our interests, we had to agree on a plan for dividing housework, paying bills, arranging a way to shuttle our son to football practice and even choose new furniture for the living room. Every decision required design thinking, communication and trade-offs that had to work for both of us.

Through experience, we learned that both business and personal problems were best solved jointly. The only way joint decision-making could work was if we truly respected and protected each other's interests. Sound impossible? It's not easy, but that's the difference between thinking as an individual and thinking as customers of each other. If you want to succeed in love, you must care as much about your partner's happiness as your own. To recharge a marriage or a business you have to consistently energize your partner's batteries, not drain them dry. Respecting each other's interests starts with mutual empathy. You may never be able to know what someone feels, but you can listen to them express their feelings, pay attention to what they do, and ask them what you can do to make their life better.

---

*Develop Your Respect Habit:*

*Pick a problem you can't agree how to solve. One of you go first and talk about the problem. While your partner listens without interruption, describe how it affects you, how it makes you feel and why you want to solve it your way. Then let your partner do the same. After you are both finished, think about the problem from your partner's point of view and each modify your solution to help satisfy your partner's needs. See if that will help each of you come up with a new solution that you both can feel good about.*

---

## Respect Each Other's Brand of Intelligence

You can probably think of an infinite number of topics for discussion on a first date—brain function is probably not one of them. But our first date in 1975 was filled with conversation about the newly discovered right-brain/left-brain theory. British psychologist Chris McManus, an early pioneer in brain research, wrote, "While we talk about brain hemispheres, they are actually two half-brains designed to work together as a smooth, integrated whole.

The left hemisphere knows how to handle logic and the right hemisphere knows about the world. Put the two together and one gets a powerful thinking machine. Use either on its own and the result can be bizarre or absurd." Alone, we are limited by our singular faculties. Together, we have the potential to act as one powerful machine. First, we need to respect each other's strengths and weaknesses. If we know our partner isn't great with numbers, we show respect by not asking them to prepare the joint tax returns or balance the family checkbook.

### HOW OUR BRAIN HEMISPHERES WORK TOGETHER MAKES A FITTING ANALOGY FOR HOW YOU CAN WORK TOGETHER WITH YOUR PARTNER.

Managing a home together can be similar to managing a business together. We have to respect each other's thinking processes and ways of reasoning, acting as teammates with one brain and one goal, not as competitors fighting for control. Raising children, managing money, sharing chores, planning vacations and negotiating the myriad business details of marriage requires genuine mutual respect for each other's attitudes, interests, opinions and communication styles. It is essential that we understand the specific types of intelligence that are unique to each of us.

### RESPECTING YOUR PARTNER'S STRENGTHS AND NOT RESENTING THEIR WEAKNESSES SHOWS THAT YOU VALUE THEM AS THEY ARE, NOT AS YOU WISH THEY WERE.

Writing a book together is a fair example of how different attitudes complicate working as a team. When we decided to write this book, we each had to find a way to express ourselves as a couple and still be able to communicate our individual viewpoints.

Former U.S. President Jimmy Carter once said that he and First Lady Rosalynn Carter tried writing a book together but quickly discovered their styles didn't blend well. President Carter liked to write with a broad stroke, then go back later and edit. The first lady preferred to write and edit as she went along until each paragraph was honed to perfection. After struggling to adapt to each other, they finally decided it was not going to work.

We devised the narrative style we are using in this book to allow us to speak as a couple when necessary and with singular voices when it is the better way to relate a personal experience. First, we talk about an idea. Next, one of us starts writing. Then we talk and the other edits what was written and adds more ideas. One of us rewrites and the other edits and we continue until we both feel satisfied. Admittedly, in the beginning of our relationship, collaboration was uneven. We had no map to follow, but we experimented until we found a way that felt right.

## WHEN THE EXPERT AND THE NOVICE LISTEN CAREFULLY TO EACH OTHER, THEY BOTH GAIN INSIGHT.

When one partner has a particular talent, skill or expertise, such as accounting, art, construction or medicine, it makes sense for the other partner to respect and trust their knowledge. That said, keep in mind that breakthroughs in many fields of endeavor come from questions asked by people with little or no experience in the subject matter.

*Develop Your Respect Habit:*

*Today, sit down with your partner and be honest about what you feel are your strengths and weaknesses. Compare each other's strengths and talk about how you can use them to make you a stronger couple.*

## Respect Each Other's Ideas and Viewpoints

Most couples understand the necessity of compromise. We want to emphasize the method we use to help us care about each other's needs. We realized that when solving problems we didn't need to compromise so much as combine and optimize our ideas.

True cooperation isn't a *giving-in* process, a reluctant surrender of one's personal desires. It's a *giving-to* process, where concern for the effect on your partner is as important as satisfying your own needs. To become each other's best customer you have to work as a unit and combine your ideas.

### IF WE ARE GOING TO MASTER MARRIAGE, WE HAVE TO PLAY IT AS A TEAM SPORT.

*Dennis:* Mary Lou admits that in the beginning of our relationship she was too cautious with her ideas; I admit I was too confident in mine. When I had a new product idea, she was reluctant to offer her own advice or opinion out of concern I would feel criticized. I was more likely to push hard to get my way and didn't listen or solicit her ideas. We all want approval from our partners, not criticism, so we had to feel our way until we trusted each other's point of view as valid help and not as disapproval. Learning to respect each other and our different styles made it possible for us to work together for forty years. We discovered early on that the only way we could work together was to promise that no matter how negative our words sounded or felt, we always meant them to be positive, never to hurt or attack. Nothing was more important than our number one priority—to stay in love.

*Mary Lou:* Dennis is an artist and an architect. In the formative days of our greeting card publishing business, when he first started asking my thoughts about his illustrations or verses for greeting cards, I didn't give him a swift reply. I was worried that I would hurt his feelings and squelch his creativity. I was raised with the Thumper Rule, "If you don't have something nice to say, don't say anything at all." We were also dating, and I was afraid of spoiling our relationship. I knew the best way to deliver my message was with an "I" statement rather than a "you" statement so I wouldn't make him feel defensive. But I was still reluctant to speak up.

I don't remember what triggered a conversation with Dennis about my method of offering feedback, but I do recall the outcome. I told him I was worried about hurting his feelings and was amazed when he started laughing. At first, I thought he was laughing at me. He immediately saw how I was taking his response, and he told me not to worry, that he didn't want me to be diplomatic. He wanted me to be blunt. "Just come out with it," he said.

His years of playing sports, listening to coaches and having his designs critiqued in architectural school made him comfortable with criticism. He separated his work from his feelings, and he explained that he knew my words were directed at the work, not at him. Once I understood this, it helped me feel confident sharing my thoughts. This also helped me in dealing with my students and fellow professionals to frame my critiques so it was clear that I was talking about their work and not about them. This feeling that it was okay to say what was on my mind helped me when developing new products.

**Dennis:** I agree that it is vital for couples to be straightforward and honest with each other, but not by attacking one another like political rivals. That's a recipe for disaster. When Mary Lou speaks, she always says something helpful. My challenge is listening carefully to be sure I understand. Here's an example of how we created a new product by listening to each other's opposing ideas. The product we created is called *The Vent Filter.*® It's an air filter that fits in the room vent rather than the furnace.

One day Mary Lou asked me, "Do you think we need to change the air filters in the furnace?" We hadn't formalized whose job it was to change furnace filters. It occurred to me that if the air filter was designed to go in the floor vent, rather than the furnace, it would be a lot easier to replace. I started thinking, *what if furnace filters were as easy to change as coffee filters?* Then Mary Lou could do it, and I wouldn't have to. Brilliant!

That's how our new product was born. Mary Lou liked the idea and immediately added that the filter could also keep food and other junk from falling down through the vents into the air ducts. I thought that was a great added benefit, but because I have pretty severe allergies, I thought the prime benefit was filtering the air.

To test her intuition about the filter being a safety net, Mary Lou called a few heating and air conditioning companies to learn what they thought of the idea. In the process, she discovered that recovering jewelry and other valuables that fall through the metal floor vent into the air duct is a prime reason women call service companies. I still felt, however, that the key benefit was filtering the air.

About this time we were doing a lot of business with QVC, the television shopping channel. We had invented four other products that sold well on TV. A sales group, Coordinated Strategic Alliances (CSA) presented our products to QVC and trained us how to pitch the products on air. CSA also wrote and filmed a one-minute video to introduce each product's features and benefits.

When we pitched The Vent Filter to our CSA partners, they were skeptical. They lived in New York where forced-air heating systems in older homes are uncommon. We researched the market and showed them that approximately 30 million homes had room floor vents that could accommodate The Vent Filter. They still didn't like the product, but because we had a successful track record, CSA persuaded QVC to give us twelve minutes of airtime.

Anyone who has developed a new product, made a movie, written a book, or painted a picture knows the only way to find out if a new idea will sell is to let customers vote with their hard-earned money. Was The Vent Filter's benefit of being easy to change and filter the air the one we should pitch on QVC, or was the prime benefit preventing valuables from falling through the floor vent into the air duct? Mary Lou and I agreed to test both benefits to see which one resonated most with viewers.

CSA's prop designer mocked up a cross-section of a typical hardwood floor with a cutaway view showing the air vent and standard metal grate. This made it easy for Mary Lou and the QVC host to show viewers how to remove the metal grate and wedge The Vent Filter into the duct.

Here was our plan. During the first six minutes of our allotted twelve minutes air time, Mary Lou would talk about allergies and stress the benefit of an in-room air filter. She would show how easy it is to remove the floor grate and install The Vent Filter. The second six minutes she would show how The Vent Filter prevented valuables from dropping into the air ducts.

In all our product presentations, Mary Lou was on camera and I waited back in the greenroom where I watched a computer monitor tally orders coming into QVC call centers. We had shipped QVC a test order of 5,000 sets of six filters in a box to sell at $14.99. For all previous products we sold on QVC, sales popped up on the greenroom monitor within the first few seconds of our presentation. I sat on a chair in front of the monitor. Our three CSA partners and the QVC category buyer stood behind me, all eyes focused on the computer screen waiting for sales numbers to appear.

The first minute passed and no orders. A second minute flew by and still no orders. Mary Lou and the QVC host were doing a fine job of explaining The Vent Filter's allergy-fighting benefits, but it wasn't working. A third minute went by and we still had no orders. I felt our QVC buyer's anxiety building with each tick of the clock as she urged the computer to show us some sales numbers. "I should have listened to my intuition," she said. Her feelings were understandable. After all, buyers are judged on how many dollars per minute their buy generates. If The Vent Filter bombed, it would reflect poorly on her as well as us.

We passed the sixth-minute milestone. Still no orders. It was baffling. We had never seen that happen with any of our other products. The greenroom felt like the ice room. Our CSA partners were in shock, shaking their heads in disappointment. One of the partners muttered, "I told you guys this wouldn't sell."

We still had another six minutes to go. I asked everybody to wait for Mary Lou to finish her presentation. Then I crossed everything but my eyes and hoped the next six minutes would make a difference. Mary Lou had no idea what was happening back in the greenroom, but she could see the sales figures on the monitor in the studio. She knew the product wasn't selling. When she is in front of the camera, she is acutely aware of the passage of time and knew when she had crossed the six-minute mark. At that point she switched gears and began pitching the safety net benefit, telling the viewers it was perfect for catching food and other items that fall through the vent into the duct.

She motioned for the cameraman using a hand-held camera to take a close-up view of the mocked-up grate and floor assembly. In a flourish, she removed her wedding ring and held it up to the camera. Then she dropped her ring through the metal floor grate. The camera was in perfect focus capturing her ring falling through the steel grate and nestling down onto the feather-soft vent filter. Mary Lou then lifted the metal grate and retrieved her ring.

In the next four minutes, we sold out all 5,000 sets of product, about $70,000 in sales. Back in the greenroom, we all burst out laughing in a release of the mounting tension from the failed first six minutes.

This experience made a powerful impression on me. Sitting in the greenroom watching orders appear on the computer screen reminded me how vital it is to respect a point of view that is not my own. I didn't connect with Mary Lou's idea of the safety net, but I did trust her judgment. We are a team and she never gloats or reminds me when I'm wrong about a product. She is just happy when we succeed. People often talk about friendly competition, but we never compete with each other to prove the other wrong. We believe and practice the ideal "one for all and all for one."

> WE SUCCEED IN OUR BUSINESS AND OUR
> MARRIAGE BECAUSE WE RESPECT AND TRUST
> EACH OTHER'S VIEWPOINTS.

## Respect Each Other's Egos

*Dennis:* Before Mary Lou and I met, I was a registered architect with a sizable helping of know-it-all. Some years after we were married, we designed and built a home. One day we were showing the plans to Mary Lou's folks. Her mother raved about the design and especially liked the kitchen, which offered a spectacular view of the majestic Rocky Mountains.

To take advantage of the view, we designed a continuous bank of windows that ran from countertop to ceiling and stretched 24 feet wide. Mary Ann remarked about how great it was to have so much storage in the kitchen, and she went on and on about the spectacular view. Then she asked a simple question that knocked me back a bit. "How are you going to keep all these gorgeous kitchen windows clean?"

The house was on a property that sloped about 15 feet from the front to the back, creating a walkout lower level on the mountain-view side. That made the kitchen floor about 12 feet above the ground. The tops of the windows rose another ten feet higher. "If you extend the deck across the back," Mary Ann said, "you can stand there and wash the windows without a ladder."

She was right. Given the current design, I would have to drag out a 24-foot ladder to get up high enough to clean all the glass. And I didn't want to hire a professional window cleaner every time the windows got dirty.

## ARROGANCE DISCOURAGES OTHERS' INSPIRATION.

Here is the point of this story. It's not about window washing. It's about Mary Lou's reaction to her mother's suggestion. Mary Lou turned to me with a subtle look that told me extending the deck outside the kitchen windows seemed like a good idea. Being sensitive and no doubt worried about bruising my architect's ego, she only commented that it was worth considering.

Needless to say, my mother-in-law trumped my professional expertise. She wasn't an architect, but she was an accomplished home manager. I initially rejected her idea because I thought extending a raised deck across the middle of the house would ruin the aesthetics. But I hadn't considered cleaning the windows. I realized if I didn't accept her suggestion I would be forever cursing those windows. We ended up living there for 18 years, so extending the deck turned out to be a very good idea, and it actually improved the aesthetics.

When I first began designing buildings for clients, I often resisted their design suggestions. Why? Because accepting other people's good ideas meant that I hadn't thought of them myself.

Being the professional I felt responsible for thinking of everything. Not having all the answers meant I was not the expert they hired. Being a know-it-all is also a problem in many corporate research and development departments. It's called NIH (Not Invented Here). Discounting other points of view is a way of protecting our egos. It didn't occur to me at the time that customers have egos too.

Some years after the window incident I came to realize something Mary Lou seemed to know instinctively—how to care for each other's feelings. As a teacher, her responsibility was to know every individual child's needs and develop a plan to satisfy them. When Mary Lou's mother made a perfectly reasonable suggestion about cleaning the windows, Mary Lou never said to me, "You're the architect. Why didn't you think of that?"

Now, when we hear other couples argue about who is right or wrong about some triviality such as where they ate dinner five years ago, we ache for them to respect each other's feelings instead of arguing over nothing. This doesn't mean partners shouldn't be honest with each other, but trusting requires patience. Mary Lou trusted I would eventually see clearly regarding the windows so she didn't need to push me or align with her mother to ensure I got the message. I knew from the look on her face that she thought her mother's idea made sense. Her silence signaled her agreement and told me she trusted once I got passed NIH, I would see the value too.

---

*Develop Your Respect Habit:*

*Today, talk to your partner about a time when you felt they "had your back" on some issue and how much it meant to you. Then discuss a time when you didn't come through for each other but wish you had. Pick the elephant in the room that you haven't talked about but need to. This will build trust and respect.*

### TOO OFTEN WE MISTAKE KINDNESS FOR WEAKNESS AND DIRECTNESS FOR STRENGTH. BEING KIND TO EACH OTHER IS NEVER A WEAKNESS.

## Respect Each Other's Guilt

Creating products together takes a significant amount of faith and confidence in one another. We learned how to trust each other and to rely on our differences as strengths. For example, our approach when working on any new product we invented was to spend a lot of time brainstorming together. One of us might have the initial spark of a product idea, and we looked to the other to expand and help form it. Here's a simple example of how we created one of our many products as a result of feeling guilty.

*Mary Lou:* Some years ago, before the internet and email, Dennis and I created a unique form of stationery. We were driving from our home in Highlands Ranch, Colorado to Albuquerque, New Mexico to visit my parents. On the way, I told Dennis I felt guilty about not recently writing my folks long letters, which they liked more than phone calls because long distance calls were very expensive back then. Trying to make me feel better about not writing, Dennis said, "They know how busy you are. At least you write to them." I understood, but I have always felt that, for them, long letters were evidence of my love. Mom said she liked reading them again whenever she wanted to feel close to me.

### RESPECTING EACH OTHER'S GUILT CAN BRING YOU CLOSER.

Dennis could have left the discussion at that. However, we had been married for a few years by then, and he knew when I needed empathy, not solutions, for my guilty feelings. He made the off-hand-ed comment that it would be nice if busy people could write long letters that didn't actually take long to write. It sounded flip, but I liked the idea and added, "Like printing the letter in all caps so it would take up more room." Then he added something like, "How about a large print format?" Then one of us continued the thought. We can't remember which one of us asked the critical question, "What if the letter looked long, but actually wasn't?"

New products aren't always something we sit down and plan. Often they just appear out of a conversation about a problem. We could have left the long letter guilt and moved on, but we started playing with this letter-writing problem.

We were both familiar with Jean Piaget's work on children's perception of size and shape, meaning that for most people a long rectangular shape appears to contain more space than a square shape. So we thought, *what if the letter looked long but didn't actually contain any more total writing space than a standard 5" x 7" notecard?* Bouncing this question around we realized that a 4" x 9" business-sized envelope, with a total area of 36 square inches, was about the same total area as a standard greeting card of 35 square inches. But the business envelope looked larger, so we realized if we created stationery that was double the 9-inch dimension it would be 4" wide x 18" long. When it was folded in half, it would fit in the 4" x 9" envelope.

> WHEN YOU CARE ABOUT HOW THE OTHER PERSON FEELS, INSTEAD OF HOW TO SOLVE THEIR PROBLEM, YOU ARE MORE LIKELY TO ASK QUESTIONS THAT HELP THEM FIND THEIR OWN SOLUTION.

*Mary Lou:* We looked at each other and laughed at the notion that an hour ago I was feeling bad about not writing long letters and that had led to the concept of "long stationery." Playing with the problem relieved my guilty feelings and turned them into a new product for our greeting card business. A week later after returning home, Dennis created a 4" wide by 18" long prototype box that held 12 sheets of stationery illustrated with rainbows, unicorns and fairies. Over the next three years, we sold millions of sheets of our new product called, *The Incredible Long Letter Stationery.*®

The long letters turned out to be a solution for busy people—especially kids away at summer camp or young women in college—to write long letters to their folks and friends. Many of the 50 products we dreamed up over our 40 years together were created through a process of playing with problems. We all have our own brands of guilt, and we aren't suggesting that you can always resolve guilty feelings by playing with them. But unresolved guilt can weigh on a partnership and build resentments.

When we respected each other's guilt, we opened the door to resolution. If Dennis had told me not to worry about my feelings because he didn't care about writing letters and didn't understand why I was making such a big deal about it, he could have created distance between us. By taking me seriously he honored my feelings and that brought us closer together.

In this age of instant messaging and email, not writing letters to a parent may seem inconsequential. But if you recognize how even minor guilty emotions can unsettle your partner, you can show how much you care.

**EMPATHY IS A POWERFUL WAY TO SHOW RESPECT NO MATTER HOW TRIVIAL <u>YOU</u> FEEL A PROBLEM MAY BE.**

*Develop Your Respect Habit:*

*Today, talk about any guilty feelings you might have. Share your feelings with your partner. Preface it by assuring them that you aren't asking them to fix anything or solve a problem or admonish or criticize you. You just need to express it. Talking about guilt can help you relieve it. Burying your guilty feelings can alter your mood and your behavior making your partner wonder if you are hiding something or if they have done something to upset you. The sooner you explain your feelings, the easier it will be for your partner to understand and help.*

## Respect Each Other's Intuition

Over the years we evolved a working and playing together rule. Whoever feels most passionate about a particular solution to a problem will take the lead. The other partner will ask questions, but never attack, until every alternative we can think of is poked, prodded and evaluated together. Sacred cows are not allowed. We offer up our feelings and impressions about an issue until we have nothing more to add, which can take minutes, days or even months until we both feel satisfied. Here is an example of how we resolved a business problem by respecting each other's intuition.

In 2004 we got a spark of an idea that eventually became a product and brand known as Ballmania® Lip Balm in a Ball. (Also called Twist & Pout®.) This product is a solid pot-type lip balm cradled in a fashionably decorated plastic container about the size of a ping-pong ball. Ballmania was inspired by one of our earlier products called Sneaker Balls®, Air Fresheners for Sports Shoes, Gym Bags and Lockers. The purpose behind the Ballmania ball shape is to make it easy for a woman to feel her lip balm in the bottom of her purse. Also, the colorful designs we printed on the surface of the ball made a strong fashion statement.

*Dennis:* When we first thought of the idea, we created prototypes and presented them to some of our regular customers such as Bed Bath and Beyond,® Target® and Walmart.® They all wanted the product as soon as we could begin shipping. Supermarket chains were also anxious to stock the product. But it was expensive to manufacture, costing as much as five times the typical tube-type balm. That meant our ball would need a retail price of around $5-$7 to make it profitable for us.

We didn't know if Ballmania would sell at that premium price. Target® and a few other large customers were willing to test it for us at the higher price, but Mary Lou felt we should first launch Ballmania into hair salons and spas where women would consider it a fashion item and be willing to pay for its unique style. I knew she was right about introducing it in hair salons. The problem was, we didn't have any existing customers or distributors in the beauty market.

Selling to salons would require building a new sales force, something our sales manager and I hesitated to undertake. Because it could take many months to set up this new distribution channel, our sales manager and I felt that we should drop our price and sell volume to our current mass market customers. Mary Lou disagreed with that approach and argued that we should do whatever it took to develop the beauty market channel before entering the department stores and ultimately the mass market.

### SOLVE PROBLEMS BY COMBINING YOUR KNOWLEDGE AND INTUITION, NOT BY TRYING TO PROVE YOUR PARTNER WRONG.

While improving the manufacturing process, we explored both distribution channels with the belief that eventually, one would emerge as the best choice. Mary Lou continued to research the beauty market and what she discovered made her feel even more excited about moving in that direction. I studied the mass market segment and learned something we hadn't initially considered. The projected orders were larger than our ability to manufacture, and if we had any problems with initial design or manufacturing—or consumers didn't buy the product—we would receive substantial returns from our retailers.

Eventually, because of Mary Lou's research and her passion, and because I trusted her instincts, I came to agree with her marketing direction. We decided to go after the beauty market, regardless of the added time it would take to develop a new sales force. Once we made that decision, we immediately proceeded to hire and train new salespeople to offer Ballmania directly to individual hair salons and spas.

We secured a design patent and a design trademark on the shape of the container for lip balm, so we could keep copycats from entering the mass market while we built sales in the beauty market. Assembling a new distribution platform was expensive and time-consuming, but Mary Lou's intuition turned out to be correct. Within a few months, we had substantial orders to deliver at prices that were highly profitable. And we were laying the groundwork for a brand that could justify a higher retail price when we entered the mass market.

Neither of us approached this problem feeling that we absolutely knew the right answer at the outset. We resisted the need to win individually, making it possible to act as a couple, to search for a resolution as partners. If that sounds way too rational, it gets easier with practice. Mary Lou wasn't so willing to trust her intuition that she neglected further market research, and I wasn't so sure we needed to rely on our current mass market customers that I couldn't listen and respect her intuition. Through continuing dialogue, we reached a satisfactory conclusion for both of us.

**WHETHER TRYING TO SUCCEED IN BUSINESS OR IN LOVE, THE PRINCIPLE IS THE SAME. LISTEN TO EACH OTHER AND DO WHAT IS BEST FOR THE PARTNERSHIP.**

*Develop Your Respect Habit:*

*It can be hard to trust other people's intuition. Next time your partner says they want you to trust their intuition to solve a problem, don't dismiss their feelings. Listen carefully and ask questions to understand the source of their feelings. If the problem is serious and the solution is expensive or time-consuming to implement, encourage them to test their intuition in small steps and measure the results before moving forward. Show that you honor their feelings and trust their judgment. They will be less likely to want to prove themselves right and you wrong.*

## Respect Consensus

The value of reaching a consensus on any problem is this: if a solution turns out to be incorrect, you won't blame each other. If you are headstrong and unwilling to listen to your partner's viewpoint, and something goes wrong, you create resentment. Even if you make all of the decisions and it turns out well, proving your partner wrong may damage their confidence and willingness to be fully involved when tackling future problems.

We have heard others say that every partnership, or marriage, needs "one boss." We have never used that word in our relationship. One person does not make all the decisions. When we have a fundamental disagreement about how to solve a certain problem and we can't reach an agreement, we may end up doing nothing, or we defer to the one who is the most committed to their solution. We have rarely faced a stalemate on any issue because we respect each other's interests and intelligence. That doesn't mean that in the beginning we didn't struggle to find the best way to work together, but it didn't take long to discover that our interests had to be completely aligned before we were able to listen effectively. If we had clung to different visions, and never trusted each other, we would not have succeeded as a couple or as business partners.

*Develop Your Respect Habit:*

*The next time you are at odds over how to solve a problem, don't try to tackle the whole thing at once. Write down what you each are worried about and look for common ground first. Break the problem into parts so you can find where you are aligned or in agreement. This shrinks the size of the problem and sets the stage for working on the remaining parts instead of tackling the whole mess at once.*

## Respect Each Other's Independence

The consensus strategy works for marriage, but may not hold true for the solitary artist. Ray Bradbury, the author of hundreds of classic stories such as *Fahrenheit 451*, *The Martian Chronicles*, and *The Illustrated Man*, said about his career success, "My advice is to do what you love and love what you do. And that's been the story of my life. Not pleasing my friends, not pleasing any editor, just myself." The single-minded artist/genius may succeed in the passionate pursuit of his or her dream, where compromise is tantamount to abdication, but while that kind of commitment works for the artist, it is a severe roadblock to getting the marriage of your dreams.

*Develop Your Respect Habit:*

*Today, focus on something your partner is doing and find a way to praise them to show you support their effort. Show you appreciate your partner's personal interests. Being in a committed relationship doesn't mean you are clones. Encourage your partner's independence. Aligned interests are vital to a long-term relationship and so are individual interests and pursuits.*

## Respect Teamwork

It takes confidence to believe that two heads and four brain hemispheres really are better than one when solving virtually any problem. This old saying is also valid: "A camel is a horse designed by committee." We aren't suggesting you reach all decisions by committee. Respecting each other's ideas means listening with expansive minds to be sure that every opportunity is properly considered and valued. Different perspectives create more alternatives. That doesn't mean we need input into selecting each other's underwear or choosing how much salt to put on each other's food or agreeing on what team to cheer for.

### GOING IT ALONE IS A RECIPE FOR CONFLICT AND TENSION. IT ALSO TURNS OUT TO BE A HUGE ROMANCE KILLER.

Business reporters touted Steve Jobs's genius and his success at Apple.® At one point his singular value to the company had approached such mythic proportions that when it was discovered he was suffering from a rare form of pancreatic cancer, Apple's stock value suffered greatly. His importance had been so celebrated, investors were rightly worried about the future of the company without him.

Few people outside of Apple® understood what Steve Jobs knew and professed—that he was merely one member of a team. Clearly, he was a marketing master and had his finger on the consumer's pulse, but he didn't single-handedly create the company's products.

To create the iPod,® Jobs and a team of engineers and marketing people adapted an innovative music player from a company called Portalplayer in Santa Clara, California. The iTunes® music store was less an Apple® invention than an improvement on earlier services created by others.

Through Steve's contacts in the music and movie business, he was able to assemble the rights to download music to the iPod,® which ultimately made the little device successful, and transformed the way we listen to and buy music.

### MARRIAGE IS A TEAM SPORT. THE GOAL IS NOT TO GET YOUR OWN WAY BUT TO FIND THE BEST WAY FOR THE TEAM.

In their book, *iCon, The Greatest Second Act in the History of Business,* authors Jeffrey S. Young and William L. Simon observed that Mr. Jobs went through a major change from making decisions alone to working as a member of a team. "Steve is no longer an emperor who stands at the water's edge and demands that the river change its course at his command. He is now the captain of a river raft hurtling down the rapids. He is guiding the boat, but he has a team of 'compadres' with oars as well. Whether working with animators, or a thousand software engineers, Steve is the leader but now he understands that he isn't the only participant."

Everything we know about Steve Jobs's public persona tells us that he cared about what he did and how he did it, but he didn't do it alone, evidenced by his well-known saying, "Apple is a team sport."

When partners work and play together, relying on each other's ideas and judgments, everybody wins, not because there is always an objective "right answer," but because there is "our answer."

### YOU SUCCEED AT LOVE BY REAPING THE REWARDS THAT CAN ONLY BE ENJOYED WHEN ACTING WITH TWO MINDS AND ONE HEART.

*Mary Lou:* When Dennis and I work together, our first goal is to listen to each other. Whether we are buying a washing machine, a new car, or deciding how to invest our savings, we talk about it until we feel satisfied with what *we* want to do.

We each start with our preconceptions, but as we begin to express our personal ideas, we learn from each other and trust that the other's ideas are worthwhile—even if we initially think they are crazy or naïve.

Through sharing perspectives, we arrive at something different than either of us first imagines. And if the solution doesn't work, we start over, without blame, and try from a new point of view.

### PEOPLE SAY MARRIAGE REQUIRES HARD WORK. IT ALSO REQUIRES PLAY.

We can't remember more than a few times, mostly at the beginning of our forty years together, that we have ever been angry at each other. Maybe we work well together because we don't feel a need to change each other or to criticize. We like each other the way we are. And even if we don't like how the other loads the dishwasher, we don't insist our way is better. We know it's just different.

Our rhythms are in sync, so we haven't needed to slow down or run to catch up to each other. Sure, we have different opinions and voice them, but we never resolve a disagreement by shouting, demanding, threatening, throwing things or withholding affection. We trust each other's judgment and talk issues through until we thoroughly understand what we are trying to say or do.

---

*Develop Your Respect Habit:*

*Teamwork takes practice. Today, try planning and preparing an elaborate meal together. If this is something you already do easily, pick a different challenge. The purpose of this task is to examine how you work together. How do you divide the tasks? Does it feel like you are a team or two individuals? Talk about the experience. How does cooking compare to the way you solve other everyday problems?*

---

## Respect Love

Many couples tell us that they could never work together for even a day without killing each other. Our working side-by-side is not only a matter of liking each other. We have been able to work together in our marriage and our business partnership for the reasons detailed here. We love each other and deeply care about each other's feelings. We respect each other's points of view and trust that no matter how negatively we first react to a new idea or new feeling expressed, there is value to the idea and we should listen. We consciously try not to interrupt each other so that we don't jump to conclusions about what is going to be said. We agree to work together toward solutions. If we disagree about a solution to a problem, we work together to invent a creative alternative that neither of us had originally envisioned.

MARRIAGE CAN BE SEEN SIMULTANEOUSLY
FROM THREE SEPARATE POINTS OF VIEW—HIS,
HERS AND OURS. THE CHALLENGE IS TO BRING
THEM TOGETHER AS ONE.

The first requirement for becoming customers of each other is to think and feel as a couple. We all have our individual priorities apart from those of the partnership. The trick to managing both is deciding which priorities are more important, the individual ones or the partnership ones.

How well do you and your partner respect each other? Below are five Habit Focus questions to help you assess respect for your partner. The purpose of these questions is to make you think about your own actions, not your partner's.

## Habit Focus 3. RESPECT

1. I work well with my partner to solve problems.

| 1 | 2 | 3 | 4 | 5 | 6 | 7 | 8 | 9 |
|---|---|---|---|---|---|---|---|---|

2. I respect my partner's unique style.

| 1 | 2 | 3 | 4 | 5 | 6 | 7 | 8 | 9 |
|---|---|---|---|---|---|---|---|---|

3. I value my partner's ideas and points of view.

| 1 | 2 | 3 | 4 | 5 | 6 | 7 | 8 | 9 |
|---|---|---|---|---|---|---|---|---|

4. I am a good listener.

| 1 | 2 | 3 | 4 | 5 | 6 | 7 | 8 | 9 |
|---|---|---|---|---|---|---|---|---|

5. I am easy to get along with.

| 1 | 2 | 3 | 4 | 5 | 6 | 7 | 8 | 9 |
|---|---|---|---|---|---|---|---|---|

# 4. RECIPROCATION

There's an old business maxim that captures the importance of action. "Nothing happens until somebody sells something." In matters of love we might say, "Nothing happens until somebody gives something," which also creates action. By giving love and understanding to our partners we get them in return.

### THE LOVE EQUATION
### GIVE = GET

## Give Love and You'll Get Love

We believe that endless love can only be fully realized through reciprocation, the lifeblood of caring that generates a virtuous cycle of mutual passion and intimacy. Here is an example. Years ago, we moved into a new neighborhood and a woman representing a community service known as Welcome Wagon® rang our doorbell.

She represented local businesses that were offering gifts and samples of their wares and special discounts for their products and services. Now, Welcome Wagon can be found online, and local merchants are located by entering your zip code into a search box. Before the internet, the personal touch extended by Welcome Wagon created a warm feeling about the new neighborhood, and it provided valuable information about local services.

Welcome Wagon merchants offered free samples and discounts designed to trigger our natural feelings of reciprocity. The friendly, helpful representative gave us a sense of the community, and consequently, we wanted to support the businesses that reached out to us.

### THE POWER OF RECIPROCITY MOTIVATES US TO REPAY OTHERS FOR WHAT WE HAVE RECEIVED FROM THEM.

According to authors, Goldstein, Martin, and Cialdini, in their book, *Yes, 50 Scientifically Proven Ways to Be Persuasive,* the reciprocity norm drives us toward fairness and equity in our everyday social interactions, our business dealings and our close relationships, and it helps us build trust with others."

One example of this effect is reflected in an experiment by social psychologist Dennis Regan showing that people who received a small, unsolicited gift from a stranger in the form of a can of Coca-Cola,* purchased twice as many raffle tickets from him as those who received no gift at all. "This occurred despite the fact that there was a time delay between the gift and the request," writes Regan. "And the stranger didn't make any kind of reference to the original gift when he made his pitch about the raffle tickets." In other words, the people receiving the gift didn't need to be told they should reciprocate by purchasing a ticket. They simply felt they ought to.

In another case, a researcher sent Christmas cards to a number of people he didn't know. Most returned a card, and some even put him on their permanent Christmas card list. Then there is the need to send presents to others for fear that you will receive something from them and not be able to reciprocate in time for Christmas. This ritual is so powerful that some people will send gifts well in advance of the holiday so that the receiver will have a chance to reciprocate, even if they had not intended to.

Reciprocity in marketing is the basis for credit card loyalty programs, points-for-purchase, mileage programs and club discounts. Virtually all of us have been targeted by companies promising free days of vacation at an exotic resort in return for sitting through a few hours of a sales pitch. Furniture stores often provide customers a complementary bottle of water while they shop.

Marketers that sell products on the internet are expected to give away their best content to entice prospects to know, love, and trust them. If the products perform well, prospects are likely to reciprocate by becoming customers and even loyal fans.

A western-based restaurant chain, Village Inn®, offers free slices of pie on Wednesdays with any in-store purchase, even a single cup of coffee. Tire retailers compete for our business by fixing flat tires at no charge, even if we didn't purchase the tires from them, just to win our new tire business. They all know the power of reciprocation, and the amazing part is even though we know the free gift is an enticement to buy, we still feel we ought to do something in return.

Wall Street columnist, Stephanie Simon, wrote a feature, "The Guilted Age: Spending to Keep Others Afloat." The article showed how people who were suffering economic setbacks were still able to help others in need. Ms. Simon described a woman who was scrimping during the recession but continued to buy what she called exotic foods, such as humus, naan, and chai from the couple who owned a small ethnic market near her home. She did it because she said she felt worse not helping them. She liked the couple that owned the store. She liked seeing their kids who played by the cash register after school. She saw how empty their shop was and heard they had both taken second jobs, so despite her own pinched budget the woman felt compelled to help them out, spending $50.

We all have felt like doing something for people who have helped us. But reciprocity can also be used to manipulate, especially in business. This is why Walmart® and other companies don't allow their executives or buyers to accept gifts from suppliers who want to influence their purchasing decisions. And we all know the power that lobbyists wield using people in Congress to introduce legislation favorable to their interests. In our own business, we didn't allow our employees to accept free lunches, golf outings, or any other kind of gifts from suppliers for this reason.

## Reciprocity Builds Intimacy, But Beware

The need to return a gift or a favor is powerful, making it possible for reciprocity to be used subtly or overtly to maneuver and control others. We see it every day on the internet where marketers use what is called the "ethical bribe" to collect email addresses in exchange for some free information such as an e-book or report.

PSYCHOLOGISTS HAVE SHOWN THAT BORROW-ING FROM SOMEONE OR ASKING FOR THEIR HELP OR OPINION ACTUALLY DRAWS THEM EMOTIONALLY CLOSER.

Reciprocation can be carefully planned to manipulate or it can be a gift to someone we like and whom we hope will like us in return. We text and send friendship cards, make phone calls, follow people on Twitter,® "like" their Facebook® page, and offer spur-of-the-moment gifts for no particular reason. Often, we reciprocate simply because of the good feeling that we get from others. When it comes to marriage, however, if you are using the power of reciprocity to manipulate your partner, beware. Even people deeply in love can feel the difference between being loved and being used.

---

*Develop Your Reciprocation Habit:*

*Today, ask your partner's opinion about something and care about the answer. It shows you value their opinion and it will draw you closer. Listening is a powerful way to reciprocate care and reward your partner for their friendship.*

---

## Reciprocate a Passion

***Dennis:*** Sometimes reciprocation is so subtle that we aren't even aware of it. I felt it early in my relationship with Mary Lou, though I didn't understand it until years later. I first saw Mary Lou one Friday night after work when she breezed through the front door of a popular Denver, Colorado watering hole called The Lift. The bar was designed to feel like a ski lodge but its appeal was in giving customers all the fresh, boiled shrimp they could eat in exchange for the purchase of a drink.

Mary Lou is a gorgeous woman (she tried to edit this out, but I am in control of this paragraph so I can write as I please). She is 5'9," athletic, stylish with a personality that makes people feel good about themselves and the world in general. I once told a friend that the light from her smile could make flowers grow through concrete—and not just between the cracks.

I felt her bright spirit the moment she entered The Lift that evening. I can still hear the trumpets. She exuded openness, meaning she looked like a happy person that wouldn't shoot me down if I approached her. Later I learned she was a teacher and had come with a girlfriend to grab a bite before taking in a nearby movie. I was there with a few friends after work, but they were too busy talking to notice her. Lucky me.

She and her friend maneuvered through the crowded room and found a place to sit on the dance floor. Nobody was dancing. The place was busier than a Vail, Colorado ski lodge after sunset, everyone trying to talk while balancing their drinks and plates of shrimp.

Wasting no time, Mary Lou landed in the shrimp line where she immediately began building a shrimp skyscraper on a small plate, suggesting that teachers were underfed as well as underpaid. I slipped in behind her and commented that she looked hungry. She smiled and confessed she was scavenging for two, referring to her friend who was holding down their place on the far side of the dance floor. Before I could find out more, we were separated. I felt like an abandoned mutt and backtracked to safety among my friends while keeping one eye on her and mustering my courage to go back for another try as soon as I saw an opening.

The noise and where she was sitting on the crowded dance floor, made it impossible for me to squeeze in and start a conversation. Before I could reconnect, she stood, slung her purse over her shoulder and started for the door. I couldn't let her escape without knowing her name and how to contact her, so I slipped through the crowd and intercepted her just before she reached the exit.

I positioned myself near the doorway. As she approached, I smiled and told her that I had wanted to continue our conversation in the shrimp line, but lost her in the crowd. I said I noticed she was leaving and would like to call her if she would give me her phone number. She looked at me like I was trying to turn in my homework late. Teachers possess a special kind of savvy when it comes to hearing lame excuses.

She said, "I don't give my number to strangers." I quickly introduced myself and reminded her that we had a common interest in seafood. I promised to call her so we could discover other interests we might share. Maybe because of my pathetic, yet sincere look, she took pity on me. As her girlfriend was dragging her out the door complaining about being late for the movie, she said, "Okay, if you can remember it, here it is." Then she rattled off her phone number once and disappeared into the night. I repeated her number a dozen times in my head so I could remember it and call her the following day. Then I borrowed a pen from a friend and wrote it on my wrist.

I reached Mary Lou the following day and we talked briefly on the telephone, then a lot more over the next few weeks. In our many hours of phone conversation, my interest grew as I learned how much she loved teaching. Unfortunately, her job was also the reason it took me a month to get a date with her. It was April, near the end of the traditional school year, and she was busy preparing lesson plans each night to teach a course she created called "Med School" to her sixth graders. This was a learning unit for the human body and its various systems, challenging students as if they were in a real medical school.

The students became the teachers, instructing other classmates about their medical specialty. The course was followed by a formal Med School graduation ceremony in front of family and friends. This was a demanding course and it was why she didn't have time for me. But I don't give up easily. In love as in business, persistence pays.

While I was waiting to land a date with Mary Lou, I came across a small book titled *How to Teach Poetry to Children*. I bought it and planned to give it her whenever we might finally get together. At the time, I wasn't consciously thinking about the norm of reciprocity. I just knew from our conversations how passionate she was about working with children, and I thought she would find the book useful. When I did finally give it to her, she was delighted and still mentions it from time to time.

My gift was a reward to her for letting me into her world. Her generosity of self and her openness was so pleasing that when we finally did get together, I gave her the book as soon as we got into my car to go to dinner.

Mary Lou wasn't aware of what a powerful gift she had given me by sharing her passion and her dreams. Her love of teaching inspired me, and more than that, her love of life and her positive nature made me want to be near her and inspired me to want to do something to express my pleasure.

She gave me the gift of herself through her passion for teaching; I reciprocated with a book of poetry. Treating each other with reciprocal acts of care is a basic building process in a relationship. It constructs the foundation that is so important as the relationship grows.

---

*Develop Your Reciprocation Habit:*

*Today, pick something your partner loves such as a hobby, interest or sport and do something to celebrate it with them. Show them how much you admire their commitment and passion. Give without expectation of reward.*

---

## Reciprocate Without Expectation

Giving freely without expectation of return is a magical power. However, too often we hear someone do a favor and follow it with the phrase, "You owe me one!" Implied in this statement is we never do something for nothing. In the fourteenth century, the revered Persian poet Hafez wrote this about giving without strings:

*"Even after all this time*

*The sun never says to the earth, 'You owe me.'*

*Look what happens with a love like that!*

*It lights the whole sky*

When paying kindness forward, we can't worry about what we are going to receive in return. An act of kindness is not like loaning money and asking for a promissory note. It's different when we make a formal loan to someone and need to be repaid in a timely way. Acts of kindness, however, like acts of love, are gifts that most of us innately and culturally grasp and naturally return without being reminded. Demanding reciprocity for an act of love is a sure way to destroy a relationship.

In a TV episode of the short-lived series, *The Marriage Ref*, a husband complained to his wife about not getting enough sex, which he expected at least three times a week. He believed that giving him sex was his wife's duty. To his request for sex, she countered, "What have you done for me lately? When is the last time you gave me a present?" A husband who wants more frequent sex with his wife is more likely to have his need fulfilled if he demonstrates care for her. Her desire for gifts is a plea for him to show that she means more than a way to satisfy his libido.

*Develop Your Reciprocation Habit:*

*Today, ask your partner if there is something they'd like you to start doing or stop doing. Ask for specifics so you can fulfill their expectation without needing to guess what they are thinking.*

# Reciprocate with Service

Ways to express your appreciation for each other are limitless when you really care. One of the greatest and simplest forms of reciprocity is the humble "thank you." It doesn't take much to hold your partner in your arms and thank them for sharing their life with you.

Every act of service is an opportunity to reciprocate. When your partner cooks dinner, a compliment may not sound like much, but it is conspicuous by its absence. Likewise whoever clears the table and washes the dishes, or cleans them and loads the dishwasher could use a kiss and a thank you.

> ### WHEN WE TURN ROUTINE CHORES INTO OPPORTUNITIES FOR AFFECTION, IT REINFORCES OUR LOVE FOR EACH OTHER.

Carol, a woman we interviewed, says she feels the power of reciprocity even when she visits her tailor. "He is so considerate," she says with enthusiasm. "He treats me so well I have this feeling that I want to take him a gift every time I go for an appointment."

Special care creates her desire to give in return, precisely because she wants to, not because her tailor reminds her that she owes him one. Gifts draw us together, whether the offering is a physical object, a simple touch or a word of support. No gift is more important to the giver than love given without expectation.

---

*Develop Your Reciprocation Habit:*

*Today, give your partner a gift to thank them for something they routinely do for you. Make a big deal out of it so they know you appreciate their effort.*

## Reciprocate with Surprises

When you walk in the door after a tough day and find your partner—who just got home from their job—taking care of chores such as straightening up the house, sweeping the kitchen floor, washing windows, or vacuuming the living room, you may be surprised, even shocked, but also delighted. This gift shows they must care. It also sparks feelings of reciprocity deep inside your heart. Likewise, when they come home from work and you say, "I heard that your favorite team was playing on TV this afternoon and I recorded it for you to watch tonight while I give the kids a bath," they may be reciprocating for your straightening the house. They don't mention that because real caring doesn't include scorekeeping.

UNSOLICITED PASSIONATE CARE IS A SPARK
PLUG THAT CAN FIRE UP A
RECIPROCATING ENGINE, WHICH ONCE IN
MOTION TENDS TO REMAIN IN MOTION.

*Develop Your Reciprocation Habit:*

*Today, take over a routine task that your partner normally does, but does not enjoy. You might do it for a day, or for a week. Tell them you think they deserve a break today.*

## Reciprocation Sparks Action

Abraham Lincoln wrote, "At the engine's 'dead point,' even a single turn of the crank is extremely difficult. But jolt it back to life and it quickly regains momentum. Then all is well again." Lincoln was comparing a steam engine to a stalled economy and about the need for a federal government stimulus package to revive the U.S. during the economic crash of 1837. He could just as well have been explaining how an unsolicited spark of service or affection can jolt a troubled marriage back to life. The trick to revving up a marriage is kick-starting care into motion. Once sparked, we find ourselves seeking new ways to continue reciprocating because it keeps the relationship alive, and because it's satisfying to care for each other.

> WE CAN ALL BE SPARKS TO IGNITE THE ENGINE OF OUR MARRIAGE BY SHOWING ONE ANOTHER THAT WE CARE. THE CUSTOMER MANTRA REMINDS US TO KEEP THE CARE ENGINE RUNNING.

---

*Develop Your Reciprocation Habit:*

*Today, pick something you used to do together and really enjoyed but haven't done in a while. It could be dinner at a restaurant you haven't visited for a long time or a movie in a theater. Go to a museum, the beach or the mountains, or just hang out at the mall and watch people. Break your routine and see what happens.*

---

## What If Your Partner Doesn't Reciprocate?

Maybe a doubting voice inside your head is telling you passionate care and sustainable love don't exist in your world and aren't likely to. You say you've never experienced anything like what we are talking about and don't expect to. You may think that we are living in fantasy land, because no one you know acts toward each other with the kind of care that we are describing. You may even think that we are naïve or have too much time on our hands. Or you might believe you would be willing to reciprocate if it actually led somewhere, but it's unlikely your partner would ever go along with the idea. You might think they wouldn't even want to discuss the subject of passionate care. We understand your skepticism. In fact, in our discussions with individual spouses, mentioning the idea of passionate care sometimes elicited this comment: "I do all the giving and he/she does all the taking." Even if they didn't speak those precise words, rolled eyes spoke just as loudly.

It's not uncommon for dissatisfied partners to feel this way about each other—even if they do have a strong relationship. Yes, life is a challenge filled with combat, compromise and pressure, especially when children command our time and attention.

As participants in this quest to stay in love, people apparently believe marriage is worth it, however, because they keep marrying and remarrying in the hope of getting it right. Buried in our DNA must be something that tells us we are much better off living life as couples rather than alone. Research says it helps us live longer. So wouldn't it be a pleasure if we had a way to thrive in marriage, not merely to coexist?

### IF WE USE THE ROUTINE GRIND AS AN EXCUSE TO STOP CARING AND LOVING, THE PASSION THAT DREW US TOGETHER WILL SURELY FADE.

It's easy to let the everyday pressures of the business side of marriage keep us from caring for each other, and from loving and feeling loved. The details of daily life can be a drag on passion—or they can offer an opportunity to show each other how much we care and support each other. When awards don't bring rewards, when the cycle of reciprocity feels broken, we need patience. For some people, the norm of reciprocity is not so normal. It's an unfortunate fact of life that some people take but don't give much in return. They may need to be introduced to the concept of reciprocity. This is different than giving without expectation of reward. This is about not feeling used.

*Mary Lou:* Business teaches us that customers who don't pay their bills need a wake-up call. That could mean we stop doing business with them, or at least require them to pay in advance for goods and services.

In our consumer products company, I was responsible for collecting past due invoices from customers. We were doing a six-figure business with a major retailer who had a habit of deducting chargebacks from their payments for goods we shipped to them. Every month they would deduct several thousand dollars off their electronic funds transfer for some claimed shipping violation, such as placing the UPC label in the wrong spot on a box or pallet.

They made it difficult to interpret the reason for the chargeback. Their payment only explained it by listing a number code that meant nothing to us, so it took several phone calls to learn why money was deducted. At first, we took their word for it, assuming we had made the mistake, even though our shipping department assured us they had done everything properly. But as the deductions for misapplied labels became regular occurrences, we decided to take photos of each box showing the location of the label as they left our warehouse.

We made sure our shipping department understood why we were asking them to take extra time to photograph every box before it was placed on a pallet and shrink-wrapped. The next time this customer took a deduction, we objected and sent their accounting department copies of the photos showing the labels applied as specified. Their accounts payable clerk said that she wasn't authorized to give back the deductions, so I called the buyer who had placed the orders and told her that we would no longer accept these chargebacks, and until they repaid in full, we wouldn't ship them any more product. She said she didn't have the authorization to refund the chargebacks, that it had to be approved by one of the vice presidents.

I got the VP's phone number and called, explained the problem and said that before we would continue shipments we needed to be made whole on funds they had wrongly deducted from past invoices. He laughed at me and said, "You don't understand. We are a multibillion -dollar company."

"Fine," I told him. "If you are so big, paying what you owe shouldn't be much of a strain."

He complained about having to deal with this silly little problem. I said it wasn't silly for us. Unlike him, we were not a billion dollar corporation. He finally agreed to look into the problem, though we both knew chargebacks amounted to a game they played to increase profits. In fact, a few years later we met a woman at a party who had worked for the CEO of the company, and she confessed that charge-backs were a profit center.

Weeks passed and nothing happened. More orders arrived from the buyer and she told us to ship the goods—immediately. I called the buyer again. I knew her performance was measured by inventory sell-through in her category, and if she were out of our products her performance would suffer. I told her we wouldn't ship until all past invoices were paid and chargebacks refunded. She huffed and puffed, and complained that none of this was her fault, and she had no power to control payments. She hung up and we held our collective breath, half expecting to be told that the orders would be canceled. We knew we were at risk of losing the customer, but fair is fair.

It turned out she did have some control over payments because a few days later the money showed up in our bank account. When you aren't satisfied with your relationship, you need to speak up. Giving without expecting something in return is the way to spark the recip-rocating engine, but it doesn't mean you should be a floor mat and let others walk all over you. Telling your partner you aren't happy may turn out to be a big surprise, and they may realize they need to give more. If they don't acknowledge your grievance, stop delivering the goods until they come around. If that doesn't wake them up, it's time to make contingency plans. In a good marriage, reciprocity comes easily and is vital to staying in love.

Below are five Habit Focus questions to help you assess your reciprocation power.

# Habit Focus 4. RECIPROCATION

1. I love my partner unconditionally and show it.

| 1 | 2 | 3 | 4 | 5 | 6 | 7 | 8 | 9 |
|---|---|---|---|---|---|---|---|---|

2. I give to my partner without expectation.

| 1 | 2 | 3 | 4 | 5 | 6 | 7 | 8 | 9 |
|---|---|---|---|---|---|---|---|---|

3. I thank my partner for the little things.

| 1 | 2 | 3 | 4 | 5 | 6 | 7 | 8 | 9 |
|---|---|---|---|---|---|---|---|---|

4. I often compliment my partner.

| 1 | 2 | 3 | 4 | 5 | 6 | 7 | 8 | 9 |
|---|---|---|---|---|---|---|---|---|

5. I treat my partner like a VIP.

| 1 | 2 | 3 | 4 | 5 | 6 | 7 | 8 | 9 |
|---|---|---|---|---|---|---|---|---|

# 5. Engagement

Customers spend more money, come back more frequently and are less price sensitive when they feel *engaged* by a company, according to research done by the Gallup Organization.

## Why We Need to Engage Our Partners

Engagement is a long word that means connecting with each other. When you engage at home, you are rewarding each other and building confidence in your partner, providing evidence that you like being with them, appreciate their company and hope they will always be there. You build your relationship by instilling confidence that you can trust each other when things go wrong and work together to solve problems. A business will fail if the owners and employees don't engage their customers. You will, likewise, fail at love if you don't show your partner how vital they are to you.

People have told us they shouldn't need to make an elaborate effort to stay in love. They argue that home is the one place they feel they should be able to let their hair down and not always be on edge to perform. They say they work hard all day at their jobs, and when they come home, they shouldn't have to work so hard on their marriage. Imagine if a company that sold you a product said they should not have to worry about customer service.

## BEFORE FEELING ASSURED THAT YOUR RELATIONSHIP WORKS FINE WITHOUT NEEDING TO CONSTANTLY PROVE YOUR LOVE, FIND OUT HOW YOUR CUSTOMER FEELS.

While you may feel comfortable and self-sufficient and your needs may be few, it might be because you are being cared for so well you don't notice. If you aren't used to caring for someone, at first it may feel like a job. Like most jobs, it gets easier as you develop your caring habits. It becomes satisfying when you experience the pleasure and comfort of a caring relationship. The powers of passionate care help us show each other that we appreciate what we have. Engagement helps us keep in mind that people don't shop where they aren't welcomed or appreciated.

Companies and couples that find ways to engage and demonstrate their appreciation are the ones that grow and prosper. Engagement is a reward that recognizes the reason you married—to share your life. Knowing your partner's needs is essential. Passionate care is a two-way street. For love to grow, it must be given and returned freely in ways that feel satisfying to you and your partner. You give care with a hope of reciprocation, but not with a demand.

## Engagement Gives Meaning to Marriage

We often talk about the meaning of life. Why are we here? What is our purpose? We can also ask the same questions about marriage. What is the point of being married? The reasons for marriage are as varied as the people who say, "I do." We want to spend our lives together, to start a family, to pool our resources for greater security, to overcome loneliness, to reduce taxes, to comply with religious beliefs or even to have a big wedding.

**ULTIMATELY, MARRIAGE MAY BE A SEARCH TO BRING PURPOSE TO OUR LIVES. THE PURPOSE THAT COMES FROM CARING FOR SOMEONE OTHER THAN OURSELVES.**

Inventor and author Temple Grandin put it like this: "When I was younger I was looking for this magic meaning of life. It is very simple now. Making the lives of others better, doing something of lasting value. That's the meaning of life. A mother saying your book helped my kid go to college—that's meaning. Or my kid got a job because of one of your lectures—that's meaning. Or a rancher comes up and says that piece of equipment [that I created] works really well—that's meaning. Concrete. Real stuff." The meaning of life and our purpose lies in doing something lasting that makes life better for someone else.

## Engage Like a Concierge

Anyone who has stayed in a hotel with bell service, or used a concierge, knows the more they make you feel at home and go out of their way to inquire about your needs, the more likely they are to improve their ratings and their bonuses. The best concierges perform their service for more than gratuities. To succeed at their jobs they must genuinely want to help others.

**ONE PURPOSE OF MARRIAGE IS TO MAKE LIFE BETTER FOR THE ONE WHOSE SCENT LINGERS ON YOUR PILLOW.**

You take your car to an auto dealership for service, and when the car is returned to you washed and vacuumed, you feel engaged. You expect the oil to be changed and new filters installed along with the usual safety checks on the tires and brakes, but the shiny clean car is a pleasant surprise and thoroughly appreciated. When they add a little theater by snapping a towel and laying it down in front of the car door so you can wipe your feet on it before getting in, you can't help but feel you've received an exceptional gift. This kind of service is a special treat that adds meaning in a way that shows they care about you. Compare that with being treated as an anonymous number by a company that takes your business for granted. They make it clear their job is to do only what's on the work order. That's not engagement. It's a transaction.

*Mary Lou:* I really like the way Dennis surprises me. He'll fill my car with gas or grab my grocery list and head for the store. He'll bring me a cup of coffee while I am getting dressed or hand me a "to go" cup as I run out the door. When he hears our garage door open when I come home, he'll meet me at the car, get Mom's walker out of the trunk and help her navigate into the house. One of the most fun services he provided was washing and styling my hair for me after I had rotator cuff surgery. I couldn't lift my arm above my head for six weeks, so he volunteered to wash and dry my hair. We laughed so hard during those "styling" sessions that I am grinning while I write this. He became proficient with his technique, earning the title of "Monsieur Dennis" and winning the admiration of my women friends.

---

*Develop Your Engagement Habit:*

*Today, ask your partner what you can do to lighten their load and make their life easier. What can you remove from their list of things needing to be done today?*

---

## Engage by Doing the Little Things

Remember when you fell in love? Was there anything you wouldn't do for each other to demonstrate your love? It doesn't matter how much you know about your relationship problems or even how to fix them, if you don't exhibit care by consistently engaging one another, your love won't survive. Washing clothes, cleaning gutters and changing light bulbs doesn't feel like much of a turn-on, but it can be when you reframe it as a gift of love instead of a burden. In small but significant ways these simple gifts of service, of care, can retexture the fabric of marriage where romantic love has frayed.

> AS SIMPLE AS IT MAY SEEM, ENGAGEMENT CAN TURN EVERYDAY CHORES INTO GIFTS OF LOVE THAT FEEL LIKE REWARDS.

*Dennis:* We were members of a fitness club for many years before we moved. One day a new manager took over and suddenly a fresh towel appeared on every treadmill and step machine. Sure it increased their laundry expense, but members appreciated the gesture and it improved customer satisfaction. When I told the young man responsible that I was grateful, he reacted with a smile and thanked me for noticing.

This young man's brand of special attention can easily be carried over to home. Occasionally laying a fresh towel out for our sweethearts while they are in the bath or the shower doesn't take much effort. One woman told us her husband occasionally throws towels into the dryer for a few minutes while she is showering so warm towels await when she comes out. He doesn't do it every day, and she doesn't expect it, which makes it feel special when it happens.

> CARING FOR OTHERS DOESN'T HAVE TO BE SHOWY OR GRAND. SIMPLE GENEROSITIES REINFORCE FEELINGS THAT WE MATTER.

At the Old Town Coffee Company in La Quinta, California, the owner loves sharing his passion for coffee. "It's all about the people," he says. When he is behind the espresso machine he is in his element. He loves talking to customers and making them smile. Often he just listens and asks questions or comments about what they're wearing.

## NO ONE GETS TIRED OF HEARING THEY ARE LOVED.

How often do we compliment our spouses on what they are wearing? Making customers feel like friends creates success for the business and makes customers want to return. At home, caring for each other in small ways, making each other a cup of coffee and serving it in a favorite cup shows that we are paying attention and that we care. Rubbing lotion on each other's backs, drying each other off after a shower, and listening without interruption to one another, are little things that promote success. They enhance the desire to wake up next to each other and help us anticipate walking in the door at the end of each day. We are all familiar with the proprietor who spends a good portion of his time thinking up ways to keep customers coming back. How much time do we spend marketing ourselves to each other, finding new ideas that will make our partners brag to others about how well they are treated at home?

*Develop Your Engagement Habit:*

*Today, find some little thing you can do for your partner. If they normally make the morning coffee or get the kids up for school, do it for them today. If you aren't sure how they like it done, observe carefully for a few days until you are sure of the process. Knowing you are thoughtful enough to do it their way will make your partner feel cared for.*

## Engage with Loving Words

We might assume that our partners know we love them, but in business, we can't make assumptions about what our customers think or feel. We have to clearly communicate that we want to keep our customer's business. We do this by showing our appreciation with words, spoken and written.

Some of us desire to be told we are loved and we need praise to feel assured that we are doing okay and are cared for. In a loving relationship, we want to know that we are the most important person in the world. Here are a few of the ways we can market ourselves and practice our power to show we care.

- *Write love notes on Post-it Notes® and paste them all over the house.*

- *Write a poem, record it and download it into your lover's iPhone, ready for when they awaken.*

- *Use the letters from a Scrabble game to spell out "I love you" across and up and down as many times as possible.*

- *Find a love poem and write it in your own hand and then frame it and give it to your partner when they least expect it.*

- *Write a love note in ink on a very intimate place on your body and ask your lover to find it.*

- *Write a love note and hide it in the fridge.*

- *Attach a love note to the car's sun visor to surprise your sweetheart when they pull it down.*

## Engage by Sharing Time

***Mary Lou:*** One evidence of love is the amount of real time we spend sharing experiences. Share a game together, or a hike in the woods. Dedicate a day or night for just the two of you. Dennis and I regularly take each other to the movies on Friday nights and have done so ever since we started dating. These date nights are like milestones in our relationship, moments sharing a movie that we can look back on, like photographs in an album, helping us remember what we were doing—when.

We filled a huge jar with ticket stubs from all the movies we had seen. We would pick a stub and try to remember when we saw the movie and some details to help experience that moment in our lives. One couple we know plays a game of Dominos before dinner. It's time they cherish together because it provides continuity to their relationship and keeps distractions at bay for that hour.

Men: offer to take your wife clothes shopping sometime and watch her eyes light up. Make sure she has a good time. Relax and watch her try on clothes. Look through a photo album together. Ask her to go for a walk and tell you about the best thing you ever did together. Plan a getaway and surprise her by making all the arrangements.

Women: study the players on your husband's favorite team. Be able to discuss their stats while watching the game together. Buy him a video game and ask him to play it with you. If he is into running, offer to run with him.

---

*Develop Your Engagement Habit:*

*Today, set a date to take the day off and spend all day and night together as if you were out of town on vacation. When it comes to showing how much you care, the things we do exclusively for our partner's enjoyment will matter even more.*

## Engage with Physical Gifts

*Mary Lou:* Some people feel tangible gifts are the best evidence of love. If your partner is a gift giver, there is a good chance she or he likes to receive gifts, too, and not just for birthdays and anniversaries. Dennis often makes me cards rather than buying them because he can tailor them specifically to me.

In the early days of our greeting card publishing company, Dennis would work trade shows alone because I was teaching. When he came home, he'd surprise me with a little gift he found for me at the show or in a gift shop. It warmed my heart to know he was thinking of me on his trip, not just as his business partner, but also as his lover. I enjoy collecting hearts, and Dennis surprises me with hearts of all shapes, sizes and material. Some of my favorites are the ones he finds in nature: a heart-shaped rock or a leaf that looks like a heart. No bouquet of flowers could mean more to me. Love letters are the kind of proof some of us desire to feel loved, so something handmade or difficult to find can feel extra special. A gift that took special thought and creativity means a lot.

*Dennis:* On my birthday or our anniversary, or for no special reason, Mary Lou hides friendship or love notes around the house with clues to where the next one may be hiding so I will hunt for them. It's a fun game that tells me I am still the one for her.

She loves to bake and often surprises me with a freshly baked pie or cheesecake or my favorite cookies. I love the smell of the house and anticipating the taste.

When she goes grocery shopping, she always asks me if there is anything special that I want her to buy. And when I mention something off the wall, she never looks at me like it might be bad for me, or nonessential. She treats me like I am her favorite customer and my wish is her command.

Have fun with gifts. Give your partner a catalog of products from their favorite company and challenge them to find the one product among the pages that you have picked for them.

---

*Develop Your Engagement Habit:*

*Today, use Google's translation tool. Learn how to say "I love you," in seventy languages. "Es mīlu tevi," means "I love you" in Latvian. Make a little booklet and give it to your partner. Text a new one each day for a week.*

---

## Engage with Service

*Mary Lou:* In the movie *Avatar*, the key greeting between characters is, "I see you." Acts of service show that we see our partners, that they are uppermost in our thoughts. Cleaning the house, repairing a plumbing pipe, cleaning leaves from the gutters or filling the car with gas, all comprise physical acts that demonstrate our love.

Serving our partners without being asked is especially potent because it offers tangible proof of anticipating each other's needs. A friend of ours knows how much a clean car means to her husband. She detailed it as an anniversary gift, even using a toothbrush on the little cracks and crevices.

Our daughter-in-law is an accomplished photographer and artist. Our son is a successful entrepreneur and a first-rate builder and woodworker who creates beautiful furniture. They bought an old house in Seattle, tore it down to a shell and rebuilt it with incredible care. After they were living in the rebuilt house, he spent months of weekends transforming the garage into a photography studio for Kathleen. It was a labor of love and commitment that demonstrated how much he cared for her and her passion for photography.

## Engage with Touch

For some of us, kissing, hugging, cuddling together on the couch, holding hands, giving back rubs, or any physical touch and spontaneous sex are evidence of love.

The typical hug lasts about two seconds. Imagine the impact of a hug that lasts 20 seconds. Try it. American Express used to advertise its credit card with the slogan, "Never leave home without it." When you never leave home without sharing a passionate hug, you reassure each other that your love is alive and important to one another.

## Engage with Acceptance

We all have felt the need to improve others, especially the people closest to us. But, to the person being improved, advice can feel like rejection.

We can always find things about our partners that bother us, and they can find things about us that irritate them. In classical Greek tragedy, "hubris," excessive arrogance, often leads to the downfall of the hero. Arrogance, the idea that "I know better," is the source of many an argument even though the question or problem may be nothing more than a matter of opinion, style or personal choice.

Couples can frustrate each other over the simplest preferences and styles, such as how a closet or desk is organized, which brand of artificial sweetener to use in the coffee, whether it's good or bad to wet the toothbrush before applying toothpaste or what route to take driving just about anywhere. Passionate caring is about giving each other the right to make choices without feeling criticized.

> ONLY ROBOTS CAN BE PROGRAMMED TO DO
> WHAT WE WANT THE SAME WAY EVERY TIME.
> YOU CAN'T CUDDLE A ROBOT.

## Engage with Compliments

In 1933 Helen Keller, the first deaf and blind person to graduate from college, penned a piece in *The Atlantic Monthly* about how even sighted people often don't see what is staring them in the face. She wrote, "As an experiment, I have questioned husbands of long-standing about the color of their wives' eyes, and often they express embarrassed confusion and admit they do not know."

Helen Keller didn't mean this observation as an indictment of men in particular. It was an example of how easily we all take the familiar, even our own partners, for granted.

Knowing your true love's eye color is not especially impressive, but showing that you love the color can have a positive effect. It would be silly to say: "Hey, I just noticed you have blue eyes." But how about taking a few moments to look into your true love's eyes and hold the gaze for just a few seconds longer than normal before whispering, "I have always loved the sparkle in your blue eyes."

> A VERY SPECIFIC COMPLIMENT IS ESPECIALLY ENGAGING. IT DEMONSTRATES THAT YOU ARE THINKING EXPLICITLY ABOUT THEM AND THE UNIQUE QUALITIES THAT ATTRACT YOU.

Novelists create engaging characters we can emulate. How often have we read a book with a character who says something that makes us smile and wish we had thought of it? Author Robert Crais writes about a private eye named Elvis Cole. In one scene from his noir novel, *L.A. Requiem*, Elvis doesn't just give flowers to Lucy, the woman he loves, he *presents* her the flowers.

*"Oh, they're lovely." [says Lucy]*

*"Do you see the tears?" [he asks]*

*She smiled but looked confused. "What tears?"*

*"They're sad. Now that they've seen you, they know that they're not the prettiest things on earth."*

## WHEN IT COMES TO MAKING OUR PARTNERS FEEL GOOD, WE HAVE A LOT TO LEARN FROM THE PROSE MASTERS AND SHOULD TAKE ADVANTAGE OF THEIR TALENTS.

Okay, not all of us have silver tongues, but beautiful words don't need to be our original creations to be meaningful. We can attribute the words to the writer.

---

*Develop Your Engagement Habit:*

*Today, notice something about your true love that you always liked but haven't complimented in a while. Think of a romantic way to tell them. The more effort it takes, the better. Don't be afraid to copy an idea from a book. Think beyond appearances. What do you admire about your partner's inner qualities, how they act with you and others or how they make you feel just by being around them?*

---

## Engage with Intimate Gifts

The original TV show, *The Newlywed Game,* was famous for exposing couples' mutual ignorance. Once, when contestants were asked if they knew how much their true love weighed, guesses weren't within twenty pounds of the right answer. Why does this matter?

Knowing your partner in detail is a step toward understanding and satisfying their customer needs. Giving highly personalized gifts is an important way to show you care. This is difficult to do if you don't know their intimate statistics such as ring size, shoe size, dress or shirt collar size, inseam, sleeve length, or hat size, let alone their favorite color. Knowing your mate's intimate measures and wishful treasures demonstrates care and builds unshakable trust.

Imagine how valued your sweetheart would feel if she received a ring that you had sized by the jeweler to fit the first time she put it on. It's easy to slip one of her favorites out of her jewelry case and take it to the store for a measurement. Doing that proves to her that she is worth special planning and consideration. It's like a concierge finding out your name when you check into a hotel, then greeting you by name when you pass his lobby desk.

## PUTTING YOUR PARTNER'S NEEDS FIRST IS AN UNSHAKABLE WAY OF BUILDING TRUST AND PROVING YOUR LOVE.

*Mary Lou:* Dennis has taken my breath away with gifts many times, but there are three that I always remember.

*Story 1. Hidden Treasure.* When we were first married, we chose matching gold bands. I never expected anything else. Shortly before our eleventh Christmas together he asked me if there was anything special that I wanted. I told him I would love a white down jacket to keep me warm on recess duty on the school playground. That year we drove to Albuquerque to spend the holidays with my folks. I knew that a big box was packed in the trunk and guessed it was my coat.

Sure enough on Christmas morning, I opened the box to discover a beautiful white down jacket that fit me perfectly. Dennis suggested that I put my hands in the pockets to be sure they were deep enough to keep my hands warm. I discovered a little black box in the right pocket. Inside was a gorgeous gold band lined with two rows of diamonds. Mom and I burst into tears while our son and Dennis and my dad grinned. I never take it off. It reminds me how lucky I am, and I relive the surprise every time I look at the ring.

*Story 2. You Are Invited.* We eloped instead of having a large wedding, so we did not create a gift registry anywhere. At home on our eighteenth anniversary, Dennis called from downstairs and asked me to come into the dining room. He had set the table with eight place settings of china and silverware that he chose based on comments he'd heard me say when we were shopping or eating in restaurants. He had listened well. They suit us perfectly. Every time we use them, I remember how thoughtfully he chose them.

*Story 3. The Perfect Fit.* After we sold our consumer products business in 2005, we decided to go to California for a seven-week vacation. Because of the demands of the business, we had never taken more than two weeks off, so it was a special time.

We stopped in Albuquerque to spend Christmas with my parents, and when we walked into their house I saw two large boxes addressed to Dennis, standing in the living room.

On Christmas morning, the boxes were suddenly gone. When I asked him where they were, he told me to look in my old bedroom closet. To my amazement he had chosen a new wardrobe for me, complete with jewelry to match. There were eight new outfits hanging there.

### PAYING ATTENTION TO THE MOST IMPORTANT PERSON IN YOUR WORLD IS NOT A TALENT BUT A SKILL YOU CAN LEARN.

Just as a company can design an incentive plan for its employees, you can create your own incentives to reward each other. The challenge of marriage is to make the partnership into the equivalent of a great company. How? By being a more desirable product and a more caring person and by knowing what your partner needs and how to satisfy those needs.

How well do you and your partner engage each other? Below are five Habit Focus questions for this chapter to help you assess your power of engagement. Use your answers to start a conversation about your perceptions and expectations. Remember this is about giving your partner the kind of customer care they need.

# Habit Focus 5. ENGAGEMENT

1. I often give my partner gifts.

| 1 | 2 | 3 | 4 | 5 | 6 | 7 | 8 | 9 |
|---|---|---|---|---|---|---|---|---|

2. I like to experience things together.

| 1 | 2 | 3 | 4 | 5 | 6 | 7 | 8 | 9 |
|---|---|---|---|---|---|---|---|---|

3. I often touch and cuddle with my partner.

| 1 | 2 | 3 | 4 | 5 | 6 | 7 | 8 | 9 |
|---|---|---|---|---|---|---|---|---|

4. I tell my partner "I love you" every day.

| 1 | 2 | 3 | 4 | 5 | 6 | 7 | 8 | 9 |
|---|---|---|---|---|---|---|---|---|

5. I treat my partner like we are still dating.

| 1 | 2 | 3 | 4 | 5 | 6 | 7 | 8 | 9 |
|---|---|---|---|---|---|---|---|---|

# 6. EXPECTATIONS

If your spouse doesn't grumble and whine about every single thing that bugs them, it doesn't necessarily mean they're delighted with the relationship. We all put up with each other's weirdness because of a built-in tolerance factor. However, passionate care is not about tolerating. It's about delighting.

Customer satisfaction is as critical at home as it is where you shop. The secret to keeping customers happy is not merely doing what is necessary to keep them from complaining. You must do what will surpass their expectations. The best way to ensure that your true love won't want their money back, or shop elsewhere, is by not giving the competition a chance to steal them away.

In his book, *Think and Grow Rich,* Napoleon Hill advised that when hired to do a job, we should "Always do more than we are paid for." This holds true in business and is even more essential at home, where you have a chance to dazzle the most important customer you will ever have. Your everyday experiences, good and bad, can inspire you to care passionately.

*Mary Lou:* One evening on the way home from the office, I bought three pounds of salmon at Tony's Fine Foods Market, a specialty store near our home in Colorado. Thirty minutes before our dinner guests arrived, I opened the wrapped salmon and discovered it was spoiled. At most supermarkets, I usually give fish a sniff test, but my trust in Tony's and my rush to get home sidetracked me from taking the usual precautions. There was no time to run back for a substitute, so I improvised and the replacement meal turned out fine.

The real story happened the next day when I returned to Tony's with the fish along with the receipt to support my request for a refund. Upon hearing about my disappointment, the manager was extremely apologetic and proceeded to stun me with his response. Instead of just refunding the money for the salmon, he reimbursed the entire receipt (close to $100) for everything I had purchased the night before. Then he thanked me profusely for letting him know about the incident so he could make amends—and fix his quality control. That's what I call exceeding expectations.

## Customer Service vs. Customer Care

Any grocer can stand behind a counter and serve customers, but how many really care about the people they are serving? To some, service is a chore, the price of doing business. They think customers are a necessary evil and their attitude shows it. The manager of Tony's Fine Foods loves his customers and passionately cares about their needs. He didn't question my honesty, suggesting that I might have left his fish in the car overnight. His only concern was my satisfaction. Any proprietor can feel embarrassed by delivering poor service, and might even argue that customer complaints are not valid or not his fault. But when a proprietor is sincerely apologetic about letting his customer down and goes beyond the customer's expectations to remedy a shortcoming, he demonstrates passionate care.

### MISTAKES HAPPEN. IT'S HOW WE GO ABOUT FIXING THEM THAT SHOWS WHETHER WE DESERVE TO BE TRUSTED IN THE FUTURE.

The manager at Tony's showed me that I could trust him to be more than fair and his attitude demonstrated that he would take future action to assure quality. Just as important, his actions showed that he trusted me not to cheat him. A great relationship requires mutual trust.

---

*Develop Your Expectations Habit:*

*Today, think about how you feel when you perform a service in your partnership. Do you do it with pleasure or resentment? Consider how you can think of it as caring for your true love rather than as a chore you resent. Talk about it with your partner to learn how they feel about their side of the relationship.*

---

## How Often Do You Exceed Expectations?

J.D. Power and Associates, a global marketing information firm, conducts independent surveys of customer satisfaction, product quality and buyer behavior. They began tracking customer satisfaction with credit card companies in 2007. American Express and Discover have rated in the top one or two spots in customer satisfaction every year through 2015.

In 2010, Forrester Research also polled 4600 consumers for its annual Customer Experience Index of 133 firms across 14 industries. Of the ten credit card companies studied, American Express came out on top. The survey measured how well a company meets customer needs, how easy they are to do business with and how enjoyable. If these pollsters measured marriages based on these same factors, how would yours stack up? Would your true love rate you as enjoyable and easy to work with, or easy to love? Would you exceed their expectations? Do you know what they expect? Would they want a refund?

## WHY DO SOME COMPANIES RATE SO HIGH WITH THEIR CUSTOMERS, AND WHAT CAN WE LEARN FROM THEM TO HELP US STAY IN LOVE?

Credit cards are essentially commodities. How do companies such as American Express and Discover exceed expectations for something so basic? They do it with their benefits and rewards programs and customer care. But they weren't always so highly rated. They decided to exceed industry and customer expectations, and they got serious about becoming the best.

American Express carefully studied how their call centers operated and realized they had to change the way they evaluated success. In the past, employees were judged by how fast they completed calls, not how well they satisfied their customers' needs. The company set out to improve service. They thought about their effect on the company and asked themselves how the call center could help build their relationships with customers, instead of how efficiently they could move transactions along.

The reformation started with a focus on listening to the nuances of each customer's voice reflecting pain or pleasure to understand what the customer wanted. Next, they changed how they trained their service employees. In the past, some 70% of the training time went to tactical skills, learning how the computer and call center technology worked. The rest of the training time was devoted to customer service skills. Then they reversed the order, spending 70% of training time teaching how to meet customer expectations. These are the skills they focused on, as mentioned in the Assessment chapter, and they are worth repeating.

- Address each caller by name.

- Listen without preconception to understand the problem.

- Empathize with the customer's emotional state.

- Apologize, regardless of the cause, to reduce defensiveness.

- Commit to righting the problem, regardless of what it is.

- Clarify the action that will be taken to fix the problem.

- Ask the caller if there is anything else they need.

These skills can also work for you at home, especially when your partner is upset about an unmet expectation. Obviously, you know your partner's name, but the rest of these skills are appropriate.

American Express also changed its hiring practices and began recruiting people from hospitality fields such as hotels, restaurants and resorts. "We endeavored to become the world's most respected service brand," said James Bush, Executive Vice President of World Service. "That is the vision of this company." Bush emphasized that their best performers were people who had the empathy, the care, the engagement and the personality to embrace the customer even though they would never meet face-to-face. American Express also learned that satisfied employees are more likely to contribute to customer satisfaction by reciprocating the care they receive.

American Express showed they cared about their employees by offering better training and workplace benefits such as access to a nurse practitioner and nutritionists to help improve their lifestyles.

They provided coaches and exercise programs and access to dry cleaning services and childcare in some areas. Caring for call center employees reduced absenteeism, which is typically higher than in other company departments because of the intense nature of the job. They discovered a clear relationship between employee experience and the customer experience.

> ### AMERICAN EXPRESS RESEARCH CONFIRMS THE POWER OF THE RECIPROCATION NORM, SHOWING THAT BEING CARED FOR MAKES US MORE CARING.

*Develop Your Expectations Habit:*

*Today, create your own relationship rewards program. Talk about how you can reward each other for the things you do around the house and with the kids. We often set up motivational rewards for kids to do their chores. Why not give yourselves some fun incentive points to earn things like back rubs or shopping sprees for serving each other well?*

## Are You Exceeding Expectations?

How do you measure expectations in your relationship? Obviously, J.D. Powers isn't going to poll your partner to find out. But what if they did? What if you cared as much about your partner's personal satisfaction as European chefs care about their ratings in the prestigious Michelin Red Guide? Three stars is Michelin's highest rating. What if Michelin gave ratings for how well we treated each other? If you rated yourself, how many stars would you deserve? How many stars would your favorite customer, your true love, give you?

## IMAGINE IF POOR CUSTOMER SERVICE TRIGGERED A PERFORMANCE CLAUSE ALLOWING YOUR PARTNER TO RETURN YOU FOR NOT MEETING THEIR EXPECTATIONS.

How many of us would buy a marriage license if we knew we could be returned to the store, or to our parents for being bad-mannered, discourteous or impolite? What if there were legal consequences for treating each other with disrespect, indifference or even with less care than we expect as customers of a bank, insurance agency or restaurant? When you don't like the service or food in a restaurant, you may not complain, but you may also never return. Guess what? The same thing happens at home. Your partner may not physically leave if mistreated, but they can exit emotionally. Offensive behavior can cause you to shift your loyalty in bits and pieces over time in ways that you can't detect until it's too late to repair.

Marriage includes a promise we make to each other, but how do we guarantee quality and performance? We do it the same way companies do—through passionate care and by examining and improving our own behavior. In transactions with our partners, we have a choice of following an American Express style commitment to customer care, or we can treat our true loves as if they are nuisance callers. The attitude we bring to every moment together will tell our partners how much we value them.

---

*Develop Your Expectations Habit:*

*Today, rate your own level of customer care. Then, ask your partner to rate you. Ask yourself if you think they feel rewarded and satisfied to be your partner. If you aren't sure, up your game and see how they respond.*

## Exceeding Expectations Is Satisfying

One reason citizens volunteer is that doing good deeds makes them feel better about themselves. Exceeding your partner's expectations also makes you feel better about yourself, plus it motivates your partner to match your performance.

### PASSIONATE CARE GIVES YOUR RELATIONSHIP ENERGY AND IMMUNITY FROM INDIFFERENCE.

Caring works like a vitamin that protects and energizes us to care even more. Just as a healthy body makes us feel stronger and more appealing, caring makes us more attractive and more personally fulfilled. "Luck is what happens when preparation meets opportunity," wrote Lucius Annaeus Seneca, a Roman philosopher in the first century AD. Exceeding expectations is easier when we are prepared, and there are plenty of opportunities all around us to make ourselves ready.

Many of us have watched our partners suffer nagging tension at the end of a long day. They may have picked up the kids late from the sitter, from preschool or soccer practice and desperately need a few moments of solitude when they get home. They walk in the door and the phone is ringing and the dog is barking. All they want is to lie down for five minutes. When you aren't there to help balance the load, life can feel stacked against them. What if you suddenly arrive home in the middle of this mess—maybe from a bad day of your own—and seize the opportunity to exceed expectations? You have a chance to ease the tension. Grab the dog and the kids and head outside with crew in hand, stopping only for a hug and to plant a kiss on your partner's cheek while insisting they take an hour for themselves. Sound like a fantasy? It doesn't have to. Not when you are looking for ways to demonstrate your love.

## BE LIKE A FIREFIGHTER OR AN ER DOCTOR READY TO HANDLE BEDLAM AND SHOW OFF YOUR CARING SKILLS.

---

*Develop Your Expectations Habit:*

*Today, think back about a recurring problem you and your partner have experienced. Imagine your caring actions are vanquishing all frustrations, tensions and misunderstandings. Be ready to use your habits to remove the obstacles standing in the way of your partner's happiness. Review the skills taught to American Express call center operators and apply them to your next moment of crisis.*

- *Listen without preconception to understand the problem.*

- *Empathize with your partner's emotional state.*

- *Apologize, regardless of the cause, in order to reduce defensiveness.*

- *Commit to righting the problem, regardless of what it is.*

- *Clarify the action that will be taken to fix the problem.*

- *Ask your partner if there is anything else they need.*

---

## Exceed with Enthusiasm

Joan, a vivacious owner of an advertising business in Southern California, says she sometimes overheard employees on the phone with their significant others. She recalled how some spoke in terse, almost irritated tones as if they couldn't wait for the call to end. "Yeah. Uh-huh. Okay," they'd say.

Moments later, after hanging up on their spouses, they might receive a call from a valuable customer and suddenly it was as if they had won the lottery. Their voices rose with excitement and enthusiasm. "I'm glad you called. What can I do for you? Sure, whatever you want! Yeah, let's have lunch."

The boss doesn't want us filling work time with personal phone calls, but we don't have to act as if we are in pain when a sweetheart calls. Instead of dismissing your partner on the phone say, "Honey, I'm expecting a call so I can't talk, but I miss you and I can't wait to see you tonight." Which would you rather hear if you were on the other end of the call?

Likewise, don't be a bad customer. Calling or texting too often at work just to chat can feel intrusive and could put your loved one in a bad position among colleagues and supervisors. Remember, we are all customers of each other and need to give the same care and respect that we want for ourselves.

> *Develop Your Expectations Habit:*
>
> *Today, imagine your true love is a customer who can make you rich by exceeding their expectations. When they call or text you, engage them with enthusiasm. Add fun or romantic emojis to your replies to show how excited you are to hear from them.*

## Exceed with Surprises

Tim Russert, once called America's Premier Journalist, traveled often in his work. He took a page from a hotel's customer care plan to show his wife, Orth, that he was always thinking of her when he was away. Here is how she described the way he cared, "Every single time he went out of town, he'd bring me back the little chocolate they leave on the [hotel] pillow." She added that he placed it on her pillow the night he returned home.

How many of us have eaten the chocolate and never thought of bringing it home to our sweethearts? It's a small surprise and one that the finest hotels offer to show they care for us. It can make an even bigger impression on our partners, not because of its cost, but because it is tangible evidence that we are thinking of them when we are away. The reward Tim Russert presented to his wife wasn't just a piece of chocolate. It was a symbol of his passionate care for her.

*Develop Your Expectations Habit:*

*Today, do something your partner never expected. Learn from Tim Russert. Pick up one of those tiny chocolate bars and place it on their pillow tonight. If they don't like chocolate, make it something you know they like and hardly ever buy for themselves.*

## Exceed with Unique Service

*Dennis:* We can learn about caring for our partners by paying attention to how well we are treated as customers in our day-to-day business transactions. If you've had your clothes dry-cleaned regularly, you know that some people behind the counter may remember your first name, but how many have stepped from behind the counter, carried your clothes to the car and hung them inside for you? In our personal experience, only one dry cleaner ever did that. He is a young Korean man named Mike who, along with his wife, own a small "One Hour Martinizing" shop near our former home in Highlands Ranch, Colorado. Mike did it every time, for every customer. Sure, you could argue that this special treatment is impractical when customers are standing in line to pick up their clothes. Yet, Mike managed to do it. When customers were waiting three deep in front of the counter, he had someone else ring up the sale while he made an effort to delight.

### HOW MANY CARING ACTIONS HAVE YOU CARRIED OUT TODAY FOR YOUR BEST CUSTOMER, NOT THE ONE WHO MAKES THE CASH REGISTER RING, BUT THE ONE WHO WEARS YOUR RING?

Each time we extend ourselves to show unique care, we build loyalty in our relationship. When tough times come, we can draw on that equity from and for each other.

Mike's customer service at the dry cleaners inspired us to think more about what we could do for each other to better manage the laundry at home. Like many couples, we divide household chores. Laundry normally belongs to Mary Lou, but when we think of each other as customers, the divisions of labor don't need to be chiseled in stone.

---

*Develop Your Expectations Habit:*

*Today, pick a chore you don't normally do and volunteer to take care of it for your partner. Don't look for a thank you. It will show you respect what your partner accomplishes routinely and the effort it takes. Be sure it shows you are helping rather then sending a message that you can do the chore better.*

---

***Mary Lou:*** When Dennis notices sheets or towels that need to be cleaned, he drops them in the wash, adds detergent and hits the start button. And he stays with it, moving the clothes to the dryer and eventually putting them away where they belong. He knows I appreciate his help and I help him with his normal chores, such as making the bed and taking out the garbage. I might hide a note in his underwear drawer or bake his favorite cheesecake or place a chocolate bar on his bathroom counter or write thank you in lipstick on the mirror to show I appreciate him. As a result, we look for more things that we can do for each other. And on and on it goes.

## Exceed by Giving Extra Time

*Dennis:* A few years ago, Mary Lou discovered a lump behind her right ear. It had been there for some time, but suddenly it grew to the size of a walnut. We made an appointment with an ear, nose and throat specialist who diagnosed the lump as a benign tumor in the parotid gland. Benign doesn't mean it isn't serious. The tumor could continue to grow and was located in an area so close to the skin surface that removing it endangered the facial nerves, possibly causing Bell's Palsy, a nerve condition that could cause one side of her face to be "frozen," so she would be unable to smile evenly or close her right eyelid. Mary Lou's smile is like her personal trademark and the threat of losing it terrified her.

The first ENT we consulted seemed competent, but he didn't understand her needs and fears. "I've done a hundred of these operations," he told us. When he said he would have to cut from behind her ear all the way around and up the side of her jaw to remove the tumor, she asked if it would leave a scar. He shrugged off the question as if it weren't important. The main thing was removing the tumor. His manner made us feel he was in a rush to finish the consult, so Mary Lou stressed that it was important for her to talk about it a bit more. However, he barely acknowledged her concern and simply told us that if she wanted to proceed, she could schedule the operation with his nurse. We left feeling uneasy and decided to seek a second opinion.

We met with Dr. Stuart Barton at Eisenhower Medical Center in Rancho Mirage, California. He confirmed the first doctor's diagnosis that the tumor needed to be removed. The difference between the first ENT and Dr. Barton was the care Dr. Barton took during the examination.

We never felt rushed and he showed concern and thoughtfulness answering each of our many questions. He explained the procedure in as much detail as we wanted, and he never made us feel we were under any time constraint.

Each time he answered a question and there was a lull, he would ask again, "Is there anything else you want to ask?" Moreover, he understood Mary Lou's worry about the operation affecting her smile and leaving a scar on the side of her face.

He described the procedure in intimate detail and assured both of us he would cut into the fold of her skin behind her ear so that the scar would be barely noticeable. He also warned us that Bell's Palsy was a concern. We left his office feeling satisfied he gave us all the time we needed to ask every question we had. Dr. Barton listened without interrupting, without dismissing and without minimizing our concerns or curiosity.

Later that evening, Dr. Barton phoned us at home to ask if we had any additional questions. No doubt, efficiency experts tell doctors they should have their assistants make follow-up calls, but from the customer's point of view, we believe that is a mistake. An assistant calling shows concern. The doctor calling exceeds our expectations and shows a powerful brand of passionate care. Dr. Barton performed the surgery a month later and removed the tumor. Mary Lou did experience some Bell's Palsy that lasted for about three months before her smile returned to normal.

Dr. Barton prepared us for the possible complication so it was not a surprise. What impressed both of us was his genuine care and determination to see that Mary Lou would gain full recovery. He never dismissed the palsy as, "nothing to worry about," or minimized Mary Lou's feelings. He demonstrated the passionate care we all wish for in our doctors and our partners. If we, as husbands and wives, paid as much attention to each other as this fine physician does to his patients, we would also exceed each other's expectations.

---

*Develop Your Expectations Habit:*

*Today, think about the expectations you have for your partner, and those they have for you. Pick a chore you normally take care of and increase your effort above normal. See if they notice the difference in your effort. This will tell you a lot about their expectations. Talk about what you did and about expectations in general. This will help you open an exchange about what you expect from each other.*

---

## Exceed by Acting Ahead

Just about every married couple has struggled with one wearisome issue. "If you were going to be late, why didn't you call to let me know?" An element of great customer care is proactive caring.

In our business, when we knew we could not deliver a shipment on time, we called customers to alert them, to explain why we were going to be late, and to commit to a new arrival date.

If we couldn't pay suppliers according to terms, we called them and asked for an extension. We didn't pretend to not notice a deadline or delude ourselves that being on time didn't matter. Respecting the customer's expectations showed we cared about our business relationship.

At home, respecting your partner's time or their concern that something dire might have happened to you is no small matter. When you call or text you'll be late, you are telling your partner that you care about them and don't want them to worry. It's a simple reward to give each other.

Many years ago, you could walk into a department store and see a sign somewhere near the back that read, "Complaints." Now this department is called "Customer Service," "Information," or "Returns" and is often in the front of the store. This shows us they want to know about problems with their products or service and are ready to fix them because the company cares about their performance. That "proof of care" earns our loyalty.

Auto dealers have become adept at phoning customers after they have serviced the car to find out if their customers were satisfied. At home, you can reach out, too. You don't have to wait until you hear complaints to show how much you care. It's easy to ask your partner if they are satisfied with the care they receive at home. Ask them, "Is anything I'm doing bugging you?" That's easy and it opens the door to caring. A company may have hundreds or thousands of customers. You have one. That makes your care and your concern all the more critical.

---

*Develop Your Expectations Habit:*

*Today, after you do something for your partner, ask them if there is anything you can do to make it even better. Even if they are 100% pleased, just asking shows them you care about their satisfaction.*

**IF A LARGE BUSINESS LOSES ONE CUSTOMER IT PROBABLY ISN'T THE END OF THE WORLD. AT HOME, ONE ANGRY CUSTOMER IS DEVASTATING.**

## Learn to Exceed

The gifts we value most are the ones that take extra effort. We've all heard the line, "It's the thought that counts." Let's revise it to say, "It's the *action* that counts."

Shopping for that birthday, Christmas or Valentine card at the last moment can usually get you a serviceable card, but we all appreciate someone who shops weeks or even months in advance to find the perfect card. They stand in the aisle and ponder, reading every card in the display rack until they discover the one message that says it perfectly.

How many times have you taken that much care? How many times have you cared enough to design and draw or print your own creation for someone? For some people, an electronic greeting may suffice, but for your true love, more effort shows you mean it. Examples of exceptional customer care are all around us waiting to be spotted and applied to our personal relationships. Seek caring people and emulate their behavior.

The thoughtfulness showed to us by an airline attendant, a journalist, a young dry-cleaning entrepreneur, a grocer, a tailor and a doctor inspired us in simple but significant ways. Treating a customer well is easier when you place yourself in their shoes and look at the world from their point of view. The Customer Mantra is your reminder, your empathy trigger, to help you step out of your own skin and try to think and feel like your true love.

Below are five Habit Focus questions for this chapter to help you assess your power of expectations. Each of you can use a separate sheet of paper to record your assessments. Then come together and share your results. A rating of nine means you "agree" with the statement. A rating of one means you "disagree." Use your answers to start a conversation about your perceptions and expectations. Remember this is about giving your partner the kind of customer care they need.

## Habit Focus 6. EXPECTATIONS

1. I always try to do more than is expected of me.

| 1 | 2 | 3 | 4 | 5 | 6 | 7 | 8 | 9 |
|---|---|---|---|---|---|---|---|---|

2. If I'm going to be late, I keep my partner informed.

| 1 | 2 | 3 | 4 | 5 | 6 | 7 | 8 | 9 |
|---|---|---|---|---|---|---|---|---|

3. I am patient with my partner and I show it.

| 1 | 2 | 3 | 4 | 5 | 6 | 7 | 8 | 9 |
|---|---|---|---|---|---|---|---|---|

4. I always keep my promises.

| 1 | 2 | 3 | 4 | 5 | 6 | 7 | 8 | 9 |
|---|---|---|---|---|---|---|---|---|

5. I am enthusiastic about spending time together.

| 1 | 2 | 3 | 4 | 5 | 6 | 7 | 8 | 9 |
|---|---|---|---|---|---|---|---|---|

# 7. Fairness

If you treat your partner like a valued customer, will you get equal treatment in return? What if they always want to be the VIP and you have to give them whatever they want all the time? What's in it for you? When will you get to be the VIP? What if reciprocation doesn't work in your relationship?

Radio and TV talk shows, internet discussion groups and newspaper advice columns are filled with spouses complaining about their partners. Many grievances spring from feelings that one partner is giving more to the marriage than the other. They may also claim to be more understanding of their partner's needs and more forgiving of their limitations. What happens when each partner feels they are giving more than the other? In this chapter, we will try to separate fact from fiction and find the truth about who is doing more—or less.

# First, Be a Good Customer

You've probably heard the saying, "The customer is always right." For most people in business, however, that doesn't mean customers get anything they want, anytime they want it. It doesn't mean they can make unreasonable demands or abuse you. It's not okay for a customer to shout at you or cheat you.

In business, if a customer wants to return a purchase and demands double their money back, are they right? Of course not. In our company, "the customer is always right" meant that customers had the right to feel however they wanted, and they deserved our respect and to have their concerns addressed. But they were not right to abuse or take advantage of us. That also goes for partners in a marriage or any committed relationship. When you abuse, you lose.

Let's face it, suppliers and their customers can be adversarial. For instance, when one party, a large corporation, controls the power, its agents can make demands that feel unfair to suppliers. Both parties mistrust each other and work hard to gain the upper hand. This sets the table for contention.

Anyone who has negotiated from a position of weakness knows how it feels to be at the mercy of others. If your business experience is rooted in competition with an ongoing struggle for superiority or survival, you won't relate to customer equality. In this contentious atmosphere, it's hard to imagine being equal partners. However, in a loving relationship, we are not adversaries. One partner is not the customer and the other the supplier. For love to last a lifetime, we both need and deserve each other's best treatment. If we act like unscrupulous customers or dishonest suppliers, we won't get what we want because we aren't giving our partners what they want. Sure, a cheat can get away with bad behavior for a while, but not if they expect the relationship to last. Honoring each other's needs is essential to achieving mutual satisfaction and staying in love.

## TO BE EQUAL CUSTOMERS OF EACH OTHER, YOU MUST BOTH BE GOOD CUSTOMERS.

We can be as demanding and rude as the worst customers when we feel ignored, discounted or disrespected. A rude clerk or indifferent bureaucrat can turn a calm customer into an angry extremist in a matter of seconds. In a public setting, anger can erupt from either side of the counter; however, in marriage, we stand together on the same side of the counter so when we lash out we are hurting our partnership.

If you want your partner to treat you well, you are more likely to get VIP treatment in return by first being a good customer. A business customer doesn't get a platinum card unless he is willing to ante up for the privilege. It works the same way at home. If we want to get the best treatment, we have to give something to get the rewards.

Love is not a contest to find out who gives the most or the least, but love does rely on the rule of reciprocity to feel equity. For love to work, it must feel fair. Even if we don't like to admit it, we are fragile beings who need tangible proof that we are loved. Performing daily chores for each other is some of the evidence we seek to feel the relationship is fair.

---

*Develop Your Fairness Habit:*

*Today, examine how fair you are when it comes to sharing household chores. Take an inventory of your own behavior and talk to your partner to see if they agree with your assessment. This can be enlightening. Be receptive and it is likely your partner will reciprocate and talk about their responsibilities. If they don't offer, ask them if they feel you are doing your share of household chores.*

## Play Fair by Sharing the Work

As much as we dislike the idea that love has to be constantly proven, or that it could be weighed and measured like a commodity, sharing the load is one way we measure commitment. When it comes to the business side of marriage, we consider our everyday obligations similar to how business partners share the work. Each partner must contribute fairly for it to feel just and equitable.

> THE CUSTOMER MANTRA HELPS US ACHIEVE
> FAIRNESS BY REMINDING US TO LIGHTEN
> EACH OTHER'S LOADS.

That doesn't mean that partners should do the same kind of work. In fact, the best partnerships are built on complementing each other's strengths, not duplicating them. How we feel about our partner's performance at home is not all that different from how business partners evaluate each other's efforts toward making the relationship work. When we think of each other as customers, it is easier to achieve a balance that makes our relationships feel emotionally profitable.

A behavioral psychologist, John Stacey Adams, developed what he calls "Equity Theory," which explains why employees need to feel fairness in the workplace. His ideas are relevant to how we measure fairness at home. Adams showed that workers are happiest in relationships where the give and take is "fair," not necessarily equal. In other words, an employee whose job is order entry can feel greater job satisfaction when they know that salespeople and management are giving equal effort to their roles and caring just as much about the company's success as they do.

Moreover, Adams says reciprocation norms can make an employee feel guilty about receiving the same benefits as harder-working colleagues. Imagine how that can play out at home.

It's hard for partners to feel good about each other if they don't feel the business side of their relationship is divided fairly. Intimacy is all but impossible if one partner feels resentment for having to do more than their share, and the other actually feels guilty for doing less.

> *Develop Your Fairness Habit:*
>
> *Today, talk with your partner about fairness. Ask if they feel your relationship is fair and equitable. If not, what would need to happen to make the relationship feel fair from their viewpoint? How can you become better customers of each other?*

## Play Fair and You Won't Need to Get Even

Expanding on Adams' theory of fairness, when things around the home don't feel fair, you might feel a need to make it fair by doing something to compensate for your injured feelings. And you are not alone.

The Google® search phrase "getting even" gleans 129 million references, including plenty of websites with lists of dirty tricks that can be employed to make an ex-husband or ex-wife miserable. If you don't want to go near an ex-partner for fear of retaliation, you can serve up revenge anonymously through the California Astrology Association, which sells Voodoo Ultimate Revenge Spells for just $25. At some time in our lives, we all fantasize a moment of sweet revenge over some injustice we suffered. The problem is, research shows that getting what we want may actually make us feel worse, not better.

"We underestimate the extent to which revenge makes us fixate on the object of our anger," write authors K.M. Carlsmith and T.D. Wilson in the December 2008 issue of the *Journal of Personality and Social*

*Psychology.* The authors say that the act of punishing someone keeps us focused on them. The psychic energy necessary to fund retribution continues, paradoxically, to occupy our thoughts and emotions long after reprisal, providing not the relief we expected, but trapping us into ruminating about what we are trying to forget. In addition, revenge invites reprisal from the other party, which can quickly escalate. When we feel a need to get even with our partner, little acts of retribution are more common. One partner may complain, "I can't seem to get his attention, so I go shopping. My favorite stores are always glad to see me." Another partner laments, "All I hear at home is nagging, so I stay at the office."

"Although relationships always seek a balance, they do not always achieve it," writes Psychologist Robert Stanley Jackson. He says that some people have so much invested in a marriage, children or a career, they tolerate inequity because they have so much to lose. If a partner feels they are getting the short end of the stick, they might resort to anger in an effort to feel equity. If this doesn't get results, depression is a common consequence because the person feeling cheated has no way to achieve balance. When you play fair, the need for reciprocity motivates your partner to treat you fairly in return. However, if they feel cheated, their need for equity incites them to cheat back. The thinking goes, "If you won't play by the rules, why should I?" Fair play is essential in all relationships.

> *Develop Your Fairness Habit:*
>
> *Think about a time you wanted to get back at your spouse because they did something you felt wasn't fair. How did you behave? Were you angry? What was the outcome? How could you have handled things differently? What will you do in the future? Will you talk to your partner about your feelings or bury them? (Your feelings not your partner.)*

## Play Fair and Earn Empathy

It's easy to feel upset with someone when they don't act in ways we expect. Consider the wife who asks her husband to pick up a carton of milk on his way home from work. He forgets and when he arrives home, she asks for the milk. Her request is shrugged off. "Sorry, I spaced it out. Can't we get by without it for tonight?" In her mind, it is not a question of whether they can get by. Not fulfilling her request is evidence that he doesn't listen to her and doesn't care about her needs; therefore, he doesn't care about their relationship.

Consider the husband who searches the closet for a fresh white shirt to wear for an important client meeting. He asks his wife what happened to all of his white shirts. She says they are at the cleaners. She is sorry, but she didn't know he needed one today. He says he told her about the meeting three days ago. He feels like she doesn't care about him and doesn't anticipate his needs because she is a selfish person.

WHEN PEOPLE DON'T BEHAVE THE WAY WE
WANT, WE MIGHT MAKE UP NEGATIVE REASONS
TO EXPLAIN THEIR BEHAVIOR.

We don't accept excuses because we have already decided their behavior is a result of their bad character. They are selfish, uncaring, lazy, forgetful, spiteful, disorganized, dangerous, angry or whatever description we conjure up regarding who they are. We attribute their actions to their nature rather than environmental influences or exigent circumstances. Psychologists call this "attribution effect."

Unfortunately, we are more likely to misunderstand someone if we believe they are a certain way instead of understanding that external factors may affect their behavior. When we play fair by sharing the workload and doing things for each other that demonstrate care, we prove our love and loyalty and are likely to grant each other the benefit of the doubt. When we attribute our partner's gaffes, oversights and mistakes to their bad character, we are less able to empathize and to care about them. When they behave with malice, they lose our respect and the right to expect understanding and compassion even when they make innocent mistakes.

First, let's imagine a wife believes that forgetting to bring home milk has nothing to do with her husband's inner character. How would she behave when he comes home without milk? How much more caring would it be for her to assume there must be a reason he forgot the milk. "You must have a lot on your mind," she says. "What's going on? Are you worried about something?" Likewise, the husband, finding no white shirts in the closet, could judge that his wife is doing the best she can and say to her, "I should have mentioned yesterday that I needed a white shirt for today. I know you have more to think about than my shirts. I can stop by the cleaners on the way to work and pick them up."

## WHEN YOU DON'T PLAY FAIR, YOU DESTROY YOUR PARTNER'S TRUST AND LOSE THEIR UNDERSTANDING AND EMPATHY FOR YOUR OWN PROBLEMS.

When you don't play fair, your mistakes won't be easily excused as simple errors or accidents. It's easier for your partner to believe that accidents are the result of your bad planning, laziness or incompetence. If they believe that your nature is to cheat, you won't get much compassion or empathy when simple misunderstandings occur. Love means giving your partner the benefit of the doubt regarding their motives. If they don't take the garbage out on a particular garbage day, or they track mud through the house from their golf shoes, or run the car into the garage door, or forget to pay a bill on time, you must believe they didn't do it because they are inherently bad.

## WHEN YOU PLAY FAIR YOU EARN THE RIGHT TO BE IMPERFECT.

Playing fair earns trust, a virtue that we need to stockpile for when we face heavy assaults on the relationship, such as the loss of a job, a mid-life crisis, depression, debilitating disease or even the loss of a child. In times of stress, we need to know that we can count on each other. Playing fair with the little things, every single day, strengthens our relationship and allows us to weather the bigger storms and the surprises that virtually every couple faces.

> *Develop Your Fairness Habit:*
>
> *Today, be prepared when your partner makes a mistake or forgets to do something they promised. Tell them you understand, and you know they are doing their best to keep track of all the things they are doing. Remember your mission statement: to stay in love. Show you care about them and not about the mistake. Do that and you will receive understanding in return.*

## Play Fair with Household Chores

Business partners, often blinded by the excitement of starting a new enterprise, don't anticipate the enormous amount of mind-numbing work required to make their company successful. When we are falling in love, the business side of marriage is the farthest thing from our minds. But as time passes, the daily routines grow, and we begin to compare how much work each of us is giving to the partnership. This is when the fairness landscape is laid out before us in all its boring detail, and we either pass or fail the fairness test.

In a traditional business, the relationship between the inside office manager and the outside salesperson is clearly divided. Each has their job description and rarely share each other's responsibilities. A so-called traditional marriage is similar. The husband works outside the home and the wife manages the inside. While the business partnership has not changed that much in the past half-century, the marriage partnership has radically transformed.

In 1950 approximately 66% of women did not work outside the home. By 2000, the reverse was true. What we used to categorize as "women's work" and "men's work" still exists in some traditional marriages, but it rarely does for working couples, and especially for people born after 1970, many of whom grew up in single-parent and working-parent homes.

In families where both spouses work, roles are being redefined when it comes to home chores. One of the problems with evaluating fairness is reconciling work values from earlier generations with current needs and expectations.

On the next page is a table showing a list of household chores. Your list may vary, but this one offers a basic idea of the tasks involved in what we call the "business side of marriage." After reading through the items, you may be surprised by how many tasks consume married life. The purpose of this list is to help you take an assessment of your home enterprise, to evaluate whether you are treating your partner well or taking advantage of them. Read through the list and mentally check off the chores that you perform and the ones your partner takes care of. Write additional items in the blank cells. You might be surprised at what your partner does that you either discounted or were not aware they were doing. You also might feel some items don't need to be done, but you are doing them anyway because it is important to your partner. An assessment of your own performance will help bring your daily routines into perspective. Don't discuss your assessment until you spend time thinking about it. You may feel that you are doing the bulk of the chores and your partner is a freeloader. Or you might feel that you are not doing enough, and it's time to do more to keep your customer happy. You might also decide that you are doing more, but don't mind because it is your way of showing your love. If, however, you are not happy with the current state of affairs, it's time to sit down together and express your feelings.

| Cook meals | Wash dishes | Set & clear table |
|---|---|---|
| Wash clothes | Iron clothes | Empty trash |
| Mow lawn | Make bed | Buy groceries |
| Shuttle kids | Vacuum & dust | Make coffee |
| Pick up mail | Open mail | Pay bills |
| Answer mail | Monitor investments | Fill car with gas |
| Manage insurance | Wash car | Put kids to bed |
| Dress toddlers | Empty dishwasher | Clean fridge |
| Vacuum | Clean shower | Lock doors |
| Care for parents | Balance checkbook | Check credit cards |
| Change light bulbs | File bills | Pay insurance |
| Send Christmas cards | Send birthday cards | Wash windows |
| Shovel snow | Trim landscaping | Water plants |
| Prepare taxes | Make repairs | Check messages |
| Plan meals | Help with homework | Feed pets |
| Walk dog | Bathe kids | Clean whole house |
|  |  |  |
|  |  |  |
|  |  |  |
|  |  |  |
|  |  |  |

## Divide Chores so Life Feels Fair

Home chores aren't subject to prevailing wage rates. We don't have a chart that tells us how much we should be compensated for cooking meals, making beds, mowing lawns or mopping floors. The important question is not how much home chores are worth in time or money, but how to divide them up in a way that feels fair to both of you. That takes evaluation, especially self-evaluation.

We can look to a national survey for a baseline comparison on how our friends and neighbors spend their time throughout a typical day. Since 2003, the United States Labor Department has done an annual study on the subject. Their research is called the "Time Use Survey" and is based on data collected by the Census Bureau from households that are chosen to represent a wide range of demographic characteristics. One member of each participating household keeps a time-use diary on a predetermined day of the week and reports how they spent their time via a telephone interview. In 2009, approximately 13,000 people were interviewed.

For our purposes, the relevant data showed that women spent a total of 3 hours and 10 minutes doing chores such as housework, childcare and caring for older members of the family. That compared with 1 hour 53 minutes that men devoted to these tasks.

---

*Develop Your Fairness Habit:*

*Today, talk about how you divide household chores. Assess the time you each spend on the business side of marriage and come up with a plan for who will do what. Make sure you both agree and will follow through every week. Talk about how you will handle it if one of you falters.*

---

## Evaluate Yourselves Fairly

*Dennis:* One of my everyday chores is making the bed. Sometimes, when I'm feeling a little low on energy, I start resenting the time I have to devote to smoothing out sheets and bedspreads and stacking up the throw pillows so it looks like a bedroom on HGTV. In my thoughts, I complain, *Why do I have to do this every day? What difference does it make if the bed isn't made today? I also have to take out the garbage and clean the dishes after every meal. I feel like I'm doing more than my share around here.* One day, to prove to myself that I was overworked and under appreciated, I decided to add up the time I spent on my chores. I compared just two of my routine responsibilities with two of Mary Lou's— preparing dinner and paying the monthly bills. I used to pay the bills, but it turned out I wasn't as good with details or timing as Mary Lou. She does a much better job.

Making our bed takes me about 5 minutes a day. I thought it was more like an hour until I timed it. I do this every day, so it amounts to about 2.5 hours each month, but it feels longer. I think that's because I never feel like I'm making progress toward a long-term goal, and it's not creative.

I also clear the table after meals and do the dishes, which takes an average of 40 minutes depending on how many pots and pans Mary Lou has used that night. I estimated that we eat about 26 evening meals per month at home. Lunch is usually salads or sandwiches so there isn't much cooking, and we do our own cleanup. Multiplying 26 evening meals per month, times 40 minutes each meal is a total of 1,040 minutes or 17.33 hours of cleanup per month. When I add the 2.5 hours bed making per month, my total is 19.83 hours.

Now, what does Mary Lou do? Well, she cooks the meals, so if I clean up after 26 meals then she must cook the same number. It takes her, on average, about 40 minutes to fix dinner. So, 40 minutes per meal, times 26 meals, equals 1040 minutes, or 17.33 hours. What I love about Mary Lou is when she makes an elaborate meal and uses a lot of cookware and mixing bowls, she takes time to clean some of them while she is working. I know she does this to lessen my workload and I appreciate this.

Added to Mary Lou's cooking is her time shopping for the food. She goes to the grocery store about twice a week for a total of about four hours per week including travel time. That amounts to 16 hours per month. What else does she do? Well, she opens the mail and pays the monthly bills, which I estimate takes about 5 hours per month.

How do we compare so far? I'm doing about 19.83 hours of work on my two responsibilities and she is doing about 38.33 hours on hers. Wait, that can't be right! I must have miscalculated. I'm a numbers guy, but these numbers don't seem right.

If Mary Lou is working almost twice as many hours on her two items as I am on mine, something is out of whack. I wonder if she knows. She never complains. What if she's feeling overworked? Maybe I should keep my mouth shut about being overworked myself and stay under the radar. But then she is going to read this paragraph because we edit each other's work. I'm about to get busted. I guess I need to be a better customer.

This little snapshot was supposed to make me feel better about my oppression. Instead, the more I considered how much Mary Lou does, not including the amount of time it takes to manage her mother's healthcare and finances, the more I felt like a slacker. So why did my chores bother me? The more I thought about it, the amount of time I spent was not my problem. What I disliked was the fact that I had to do it every day and never made any progress. Plus I wasn't learning anything by making the bed and cleaning dishes. Yes, you could say routine teaches discipline and humility, but I would love to learn something new each day along with it. Once I understood what was bugging me, I felt like a whiner. That stopped me from feeling oppressed. I now accept my lot in life, get the job done and move on. Plus, Mary Lou suggested I listen to a podcast I liked while "slaving" away so I felt I was gaining time to learn. It's all about how you frame it.

## WE RESENT CHORES THAT KEEP US FROM DOING WHAT WE LOVE. THAT'S WHY WE CALL THEM CHORES.

When we have to do something we don't like, it's easy to feel put upon, and no doubt most everyone feels that way from time to time. Some time management experts advise starting the day by first eliminating the tasks we least enjoy so we can devote full energy and attention to what excites us. Mark Twain said it best, "Eat a live frog first thing in the morning and nothing worse will happen to you the rest of the day."

At some point in marriage, we have to reach an understanding that the more we help each other with the business side of marriage, the more energy we have to do what we love, together.

*Mary Lou:* When we married, Dennis made me a promise that he has always kept. He swore never to do another day of yard work. I appreciated knowing this ahead of time, so I never expected him to do it. I managed the smaller maintenance tasks such as planting flowers, weeding and fertilizing the beds. However, I wasn't keen on mowing.

Our son, Dennis Jr., took care of it when he was a teenager. Later I hired a mowing service, instead of expecting Dennis Sr. to do it. Listen when your partner tells you they hate doing something. It cuts down on the power struggles.

It is vital not to label tasks as "men's work" or "women's work." That doesn't mean some jobs won't feel like one or the other because we are programmed by our culture. If you think of your partner as a customer you are trying to satisfy, and whose business you want to keep, you must do what is necessary to keep them interested in your product—you.

> *Develop Your Fairness Habit:*
>
> *Today, list each other's chores and estimate the time each one takes in a week or a month. The amount of time is not as important as whether it feels fair and equitable. If you hate doing a chore and your partner doesn't mind doing it, then maybe you can trade. Talk it over and share your thoughts to prevent feeling disrespected or misunderstood.*

## America's Attitudes Toward Housework

Most Americans still believe in the traditional division of household labor between husbands and wives. Same-sex couples think the more masculine partner and the more feminine partner should generally be responsible for stereotypically male and female chores. These are findings from the study titled, *Making Money, Doing Gender, or Being Essentialist? Partner Characteristics and Americans' Attitudes Toward Housework.* The study examined responses from a nationally representative survey of more than 1,000 adults in 2015 to determine which characteristics, including relative income, masculine or feminine traits, and sex, shape Americans' ideas about how married couples should divide household labor—including indoor and outdoor chores, as well as childcare.

"This is the first study that looks at Americans' beliefs about how partners *should* divide chores and childcare tasks," said Natasha Quadlin, the lead author of the study and a doctoral student in sociology at Indiana University. Each respondent in the study was randomly assigned a description of a heterosexual or same-sex couple. The description included information about each partner's occupation and income, as well as his or her hobbies and interests, which cued whether the partner had traditionally masculine or feminine traits. The respondents also received a list of chores and childcare-related tasks to assign between the two partners.

Quadlin and co-author Long Doan, an assistant professor of sociology at the University of Maryland, found that among heterosexual couples, partner sex differences had the strongest overall effect on the assignment of chores and childcare. "Nearly three-quarters of our respondents thought the female partners in heterosexual couples should be responsible for cooking, doing laundry, cleaning the house, and buying groceries," Quadlin said. "In addition, nearly 90% of our respondents thought that heterosexual men should be responsible for automobile maintenance and outdoor chores. Regardless of the partner's relative income or gendered hobbies and interests, our respondents gravitated toward the person's sex instead."

When respondents were asked to assign tasks between same-sex partners, traditionally female chores were generally given to the more feminine partner, and traditionally male tasks were typically assigned to the more masculine partner. According to the researchers, 66% of respondents believed the more feminine partner should be responsible for buying groceries, 61% felt that partner should cook, and 58% thought that partner should clean the house and do the laundry. On the other hand, 67% of respondents believed that the more masculine partner should handle automobile maintenance and outdoor chores. "Even in same-sex couples where there aren't sex differences between partners, people use gender differences as a way to approximate sex differences," Quadlin said.

**Dennis:** This study reveals cultural expectations toward chores; however, it doesn't mean that any particular couple can't have their own way of dividing chores. Every business has a variety of job types. It's often difficult to say which one is harder than another, but we can say we dislike some more than others, and that some are a better fit with our individual skills.

Division of labor for Mary Lou and me is based more on the chores we would rather do, though it took experimentation. Like most things in life, picking chores involves trade-offs. We work harder doing what we enjoy, so we don't have to do as much of what we don't enjoy. In our marriage, I make the bed because Mary Lou dislikes it more than I do. She makes the meals because cooking is a creative outlet for her, and I find it takes too much planning. I'm a better dishwasher than a cook. Like many working couples, we hire someone to clean the house. We spend a lot of time in the business so when we have a chance to be home together, we don't want to devote our energies to cleaning. We couldn't always afford to pay for cleaning. In the early years of our marriage, we both kept up the house, though Mary Lou did more. My regular excuse was that I always had a business project to work on. The Customer Mantra changed my thinking. I came to understand that my favorite customer valued a clean house. That simple change in awareness, that she was my customer, prompted me to change my attitude about helping more around the house, just as she adapted to my customer needs.

## Fair Play and Confirmation Bias

**Dennis:** In business, accountants audit the company's financial health to be sure that owners aren't fooling themselves about revenue, expenses and profitability. Accountants are independent, allowing them to render an honest appraisal. In marriage, we have to judge each other's performance. Unfortunately, our assessments may involve conjecture supported by wishful thinking, not data. It is easy to be fooled by confirmation bias, a trick of the mind, like attribution effect. It makes us see what we want to see. When we feel we are working harder than our partners, we might seek evidence to support this feeling but also exclude contradictory facts. For instance, when considering Mary Lou's chores, I could exclude her grocery shopping, reasoning falsely that it's a separate, unrelated task. Even if I had measured it as a different chore, it still takes her time.

We can deny our biases, but they are usually evident to our friends and especially to our partners. The first step to escaping a bias is admitting that it exists. Consider the experience of Al Michaels, a sportscaster for NFL® football. He once said in an interview that fans accused him of being biased in his broadcast. He responded by explaining that after each game the TV network receives an almost equal number of letters from football fans of opposing teams claiming that the announcers were clearly favoring the other team.

Most fans have experienced this feeling because we have an intense emotional investment in our teams. When a referee's call doesn't go our way, we are convinced they are biased. Even if the instant replay proved the call was correct, evidence might not be enough to dissuade our steadfast belief that we were wronged. And pity the hometown fan in the room that agrees with the referee's seemingly bad call. We think he must be blind or worse—disloyal.

When we are in a hurry to get somewhere and have to go through a long checkout line at the supermarket or through airport security, it seems that every line is moving except ours. It never fails. We always end up in the slowest one. When we are running late for work or for an appointment, the traffic lights are always red, confirming our belief that the city's traffic department needs to time the lights better.

Likewise, when we feel overworked and under-appreciated, nobody ever pitches in to help. The cell phone always runs out of power when we need it most. The computer always crashes just before we've saved our files. That is our confirmation bias at work.

During these stressful moments, it's easy to feel that life conspires against you, so you look for evidence to support your feelings. Confirmation bias can be a serious detriment to reaching agreement on how to share routine chores. If you see each other as customers, and work to be sure you satisfy each other's needs, everything is more likely to feel fair. Below are five Habit Focus questions for this chapter to help you assess your sense of fairness. The purpose of these questions is to make you think about your own level of care, not your partner's care. Use your answers to start a conversation about your perceptions and expectations. Remember this is about giving your partner the kind of customer care they need.

## Habit Focus 7. FAIRNESS

1. I do my share of work around the house.

| 1 | 2 | 3 | 4 | 5 | 6 | 7 | 8 | 9 |
|---|---|---|---|---|---|---|---|---|

2. I show empathy for my partner's worries.

| 1 | 2 | 3 | 4 | 5 | 6 | 7 | 8 | 9 |
|---|---|---|---|---|---|---|---|---|

3. I don't have any biases toward my partner.

| 1 | 2 | 3 | 4 | 5 | 6 | 7 | 8 | 9 |
|---|---|---|---|---|---|---|---|---|

4. I don't compare my effort with my partner's.

| 1 | 2 | 3 | 4 | 5 | 6 | 7 | 8 | 9 |
|---|---|---|---|---|---|---|---|---|

5. I always give my partner the benefit of the doubt.

| 1 | 2 | 3 | 4 | 5 | 6 | 7 | 8 | 9 |
|---|---|---|---|---|---|---|---|---|

# 8. TRUST

When Mary Lou wants to buy new clothes, she often asks me to go shopping with her. She says, "I want to be sure you like it because you will have to look at it the most." I enjoy this because I get my own private fashion show with the person I consider the most beautiful woman on the planet. Plus, being in the product design business, I am curious about new styles, colors and fabrics. The problem is, I don't like to spend money.

When Mary Lou is ready to try on the selected clothes, I find a seat and wait for the show. At some point, I confess, I might worry more about the mounting bill than about how the clothes look. I hate to admit that I can't afford something, and it's hard to be less than delighted without sounding like a cheapskate. This is especially hard when Mary Lou comes out looking great in an expensive piece. I used to catch myself saying I didn't like some outfit instead of declaring it was too expensive. Once I realized what was going on in my head, we talked about it and I stopped worrying. Now I say exactly what I feel. When I like what she is trying on I say so, and when I don't like it, I say that too. When she finishes trying everything on, we talk and decide what we can afford and how to narrow down the final choices. Sometimes it amounts to several items and sometimes maybe only one, or even none. More importantly, by being honest, we trust each other. She knows I will be forthright in my appraisal, and I know she will be realistic about what we can spend.

If I turn thumbs down on everything she tries on because I am worried about spending money, she might think that she, and not the clothes, is the problem. Trust requires us to be honest with ourselves about what we are feeling and to share that with our partners.

By imagining Mary Lou is my customer, I must be more concerned about her interests than about my own. If I were a salesperson motivated by a commission, and I told her everything she tried on looked gorgeous when it didn't, she might sense I was trying to make a sale rather than satisfy her needs. She would lose trust in my judgment.

*Develop Your Trust Habit:*

*Today, focus on your motives. Think about why you do the things you do related to money, relatives, hobbies or any sensitive topics. If you feel conflicted about your choices, be honest with your partner, so they know exactly how you feel. Your partner won't have to guess why you made the choice and will trust you are not hiding something, especially your fears and guilty desires.*

## Trust Is Like Rubber Cement

This may seem like a weird analogy, but for anyone who has ever used rubber cement, you know how valuable it is. Elementary school teachers sing the praises of rubber cement, but for those growing up in the digital age and not familiar with it, here is how it works.

Rubber cement comes in a bottle with a brush applicator connected to the lid. You brush the sticky liquid on each piece of whatever you want to join together. Let the cement dry for several seconds, then press the pieces together to create a powerful bond. Each side depends on the other for cohesion and lasting strength—like marriage.

Mutual trust means believing you will stick together. You rely on one another to be honest and take responsibility for what needs to be done, whether around the house, with the kids, how you spend money or how you spend your time.

Trust is knowing that your partner has your back. The challenge in business and in marriage is how to build trust and maintain it through market and life cycles. When you build trust, it resonates through your everyday actions.

## Build Trust by Honoring Agreements

Consider a game theory known as "The Prisoner's Dilemma." Two people are arrested and accused of committing a crime together. They are taken into custody and transported to the local precinct where they are isolated in separate rooms and questioned. Each alleged criminal is offered a deal. The first one to implicate his partner will be looked upon favorably by the prosecutor. This is the classic test of loyalty and trust, and while this particular dilemma may seem an extreme example when used in the same breath as marriage, it begs the question, *when the chips are down, can we trust our true loves to be there for us?*

> *Develop Your Trust Habit:*
>
> *Today, think about a time when you shaded the truth to avoid an argument or to escape doing something you didn't want to do. How did you feel? Be honest and let your partner know the truth. It will serve you well and help you build trust and receive truth in return.*

## THE PRISONER'S DILEMMA IS PLAYED OUT IN FAR MORE SUBTLE WAYS IN OUR EVERYDAY FAMILY EXPERIENCES.

A young couple owns a Golden Labrador named Hulk who likes to beg for scraps of food at the dinner table. The couple agreed it isn't a good idea to feed their cherished pet anything but the special dog food brand prescribed by their veterinarian, but it is amazing how a lovable mutt with begging eyes can make us violate a trust. When one partner gets up from the table and temporarily turns their back, the other partner slips Hulk some table scraps. Of course, Hulk is still chomping away when the first partner turns around and catches him in the act.

"Did you feed Hulk from the table?" Both parties know the answer, but one feels the need to notice the infraction. In Hulk's case, the guilty partner is defenseless. "I'm sorry, I just couldn't resist. He looked so pitiful I felt bad holding back when we are just going to throw the scraps out." When partners agree to do something and then one partner breaches the agreement, they are chipping away bits of trust.

## IT DOESN'T MATTER IF YOU ARE PRISONERS BEING OFFERED A DEAL OR A MARRIED COUPLE WHO AGREED ON HOW TO FEED YOUR DOG, A PROMISE IS A PROMISE.

If we agree to stick to a plan, we must follow through. It doesn't matter if we are vowing not to spend money on new clothes, not to buy a daily Starbucks® or to set limits on our child's video game or sugar habit, we must honor our bonds. When we tell our customers they can count on us, we must come through.

Keeping promises is essential in business. When a company prints a label of contents on a package, they make the customer a promise. If it turns out that a carton of milk is tainted or a toy is decorated with lead paint or eggs are contaminated with salmonella, we lose trust in those providers and even become suspicious of all manufacturing. We even mistrust the system of government rules and regulations that are meant to protect us from shady business practices.

When a company announces they will pay a dividend on their stock this quarter, we rely on that promise to decide if we want to become shareholders. If management suddenly decides to discontinue dividends, we lose trust in the company's ability to forecast revenues. When we promise to take time off from work to attend our child's soccer game or school play, and then say we are too busy, our partner and our child lose trust regardless of the circumstances.

Our family begins to wonder if they can trust any of our promises. How do they know when to trust? In the Old West, people were proud of saying that a man's word was his bond, implying that he could be trusted to do what he said. Our actions alone prove whether we are reliable.

Stockbrokers warn investors that past performance is no guarantee of future performance. However, it *is* human nature to believe how someone acted in the past is a good predictor of their future behavior. This is why the routine we experience after settling into family life is often a surprise. We acted so differently with each other when we were dating.

During courtship, our actions proclaimed, "You are the most import-ant person in my life." We expect passionate care will be the way of the future, but when life doesn't turn out as expected, we lose trust in our partner to deliver on their promises. Even our self-confidence is damaged, and we question our ability to pick the right partner.

---

*Develop Your Trust Habit:*

*Today, when you promise something, be sure you can deliver. Think before you commit. If you feel pressured to make a promise but aren't certain you can deliver, explain why you don't feel comfortable about making the promise. Don't promise something, even reluctantly, then not follow through.*

---

## Trust Builders and Trust Busters

Trust is built on positive evidence. When a waiter takes orders from a table of six people, without writing down a single word, diners may doubt he will get everything right. Later, when the various dishes are served without a hitch, everyone is pleasantly surprised. When each person at the table raves about the presentation and taste of their food, trust in the chef and in the management is added. When the owner comes to the table and tells each patron that he appreciates them for coming to his restaurant, trust increases even more. Finally, when the owner offers to buy everyone dessert, we trust that this is a superior restaurant because we have the evidence.

A restaurateur's greatest challenge is maintaining a superior level of service and growing trust with every visit. Building trust by demon-strating reliability is one of the secrets to growing a business, and it is an equally powerful force for proving to our partners we are worth their emotional investment.

## Doubt Destroys Trust

The reciprocity norm asserts that a favor done generates a favor in return. Acting toward each other in trusting ways strengthens bonds of intimacy and love. When we act toward our partner with suspicion, doubt and mistrust, we corrupt the relationship and damage our chances of earning the same trust we crave.

A woman feared her husband was having an affair so she hired a private detective. The detective asked her why she suspected her husband's infidelity. She explained, "He stays late at the office almost every night, but when I call he doesn't answer." The detective suggested that he might be working hard and doesn't want to be disturbed. He asked the woman if there was any other reason why she suspected her husband might be cheating. "Yes," she said as if it were obvious, "because that's what men do."

CONFIRMATION BIAS NEVER LETS THE TRUTH
GET IN THE WAY OF OUR DEEPLY HELD BELIEFS.

So the detective took the assignment and followed the husband for a few weeks. Eventually, he reported back to the woman that she had nothing to worry about. Her husband really was working late every night.

After she read the detective's report, she told him she was disappointed in his work and complained that he was lying. The detective calmly asked her why she thought he would lie. She looked him straight in the eye and said, "Because that's what men do."

## Understanding Builds Trust

The anthropologist, Edward T. Hall, worked extensively with the U.S. State Department helping diplomats understand the cultures where they lived and worked. In his book *The Silent Language,* he cited a trust problem between the Americans and Greeks while negotiating a trade agreement. Despite the Americans' efforts to conclude the agreements, they met with resistance and suspicion from the Greeks. As it turned out, there were two reasons for the stalemate. Americans pride themselves on being outspoken and forthright, yet these same qualities are regarded as a liability by the Greeks who consider it a lack of finesse, which the Greeks deplore.

Second, the unspoken rule for meetings in the United States is to limit the length of meetings according to a schedule and to reach agreements on general principles first, delegating the drafting of details to subordinates.

The Greeks regarded this practice as a device to pull the wool over their eyes. Greek custom calls for working out details in front of all concerned, which necessitates continuing meetings as long as necessary and not being bound by a schedule. Mistrusting each other's negotiating styles caused serious impediments to reaching an accord.

## WE MUST SHOW TRUST
## TO EARN IT.

We must understand our partner's communication style. Someone who grows up in a highly expressive Italian or Greek family, for instance, might find it hard to understand the less expressive ways of a Northern European family.

When one partner is raised in a culture where everyone prides themselves on speaking their minds, it may seem exciting and liberating to someone raised in a culture where feelings are buried. However, what seems honest and energizing at first may become wearing once the novelty has worn off and cultural style takes over. Trust must be built through acceptance and understanding of each other's cultural values.

*Dennis:* I was raised in a family of five kids including four boys. Chaos was the norm and loud arguments were common. Mary Lou is an only child. She was raised in a more serene household and had no one to battle for resources or privacy. As a result, I had to learn how to communicate by listening to her and being less aggressive than I would when arguing about batting averages with my brothers. I spent my childhood and early adult life competing in sports where striving for dominance is the norm. My style didn't work in our marriage. On the other hand, Mary Lou had to learn how to feel okay about disagreeing with me.

When I understood her communication needs, I softened my aggressiveness. When she learned my style, she became more comfortable with conflict.

## ACCOMMODATING EACH OTHER'S STYLES SHOWS RESPECT AND BUILDS TRUST.

The following news story shows how insults, whether intended or inadvertent, can damage trust. Israel's deputy foreign minister summoned the Turkish ambassador to his office to complain about a TV show that aired on Turkish television. After the diplomats met, the Turkish ambassador demanded an apology for being insulted by Israel's foreign minister.

The offense: the Turkish ambassador received no handshake upon arrival and was forced to wait while sitting on a low sofa. This perceived slight created tensions between the two governments. To smooth things over, Israel had to formally apologize for the insult.

Was the insult intended, or a simple misunderstanding? Regardless, as a result, both diplomats no longer trusted the other, making future conflict inevitable. It's no different for marriage partners. If we don't trust each other, we can always find reasons to feel insulted or to be insulting because we are insensitive to each other's needs and expectations.

Name-calling, throwing insults, casting slights or negative innu-endos are trust busters in business and at home. No matter how harmless you think a little sarcasm may be toward your partner, negatives don't help you build trust. Would you do business with someone who insulted you?

## Build Trust by Respecting Territories

It is not easy to trust when interests are misinterpreted or misaligned as in Hall's example of the American and Greek negotiations. The parties had similar goals, but ignorance of each other's styles cast suspicion on motives. We all feel frustration when we are convinced we know the best way to do something, and we insist on helping our partners do it the best way, which is our way, even though they feel the same conviction for their way. Disagreements over the best way to wash dishes, keep a clean desk or how to drive the car are just a few of the territorial imperatives that will never be resolved by insist-ing on a right or wrong way to accomplish a task.

> MANY OF OUR BEHAVIORS ARE ARBITRARY AND HAVE NOTHING TO DO WITH CORRECTNESS. THEY'RE MERELY WHAT FEELS COMFORTABLE.

Respecting territory and privacy is another trust builder. Husbands don't rummage through their wives' purses, nor do women rifle their husbands' wallets without their permission. No one instructed us this is taboo, but our intuition tells us it's private territory. Bound-aries need to be set but can create conflict when we need to share a territory, or when we impose our behavioral styles on our partners. Understanding and accepting each other's different ways shows care and respect and provides evidence of love.

Many couples share a space for working at home or share a single computer but have different concepts of order and use. One partner may organize every document in a folder, labeled and filed alphabetically inside a cabinet or computer hard drive. The other partner may make piles and use only one folder for everything they store on the computer.

### THE HOME OFFICE AND THE KITCHEN ARE BREEDING GROUNDS FOR TERRITORIAL TENSIONS.

One partner prefers a clean desktop with a place for everything and everything in its place. We call this detailed person a filer. The other partner is an abstract organizer creating paper piles rising like the New York City skyline from tabletop or floor and scattered randomly inside the computer. We call him a stacker.

A filer classifies and stores information according to something like the Dewey Decimal System used in libraries. A stacker relies on visual memory to know where documents are stored and displays mentalist powers when retrieving something from a tower of paper that no one else on the planet could fathom.

**Dennis:** I confess to being a stacker. Mary Lou is a filer. Our differing modes could make each other crazy if we didn't practice a "love and let love" philosophy. We don't criticize each other for how differently we do things. In fact, we rely on our differences to multiply our resources. We depend on each other's strengths to expand our opportunities. We could complain about each other's ways of filing or stacking, but we recognize that our different styles are a reflection of who we are and how we perceive the world around us.

### A KEY TO MARITAL BLISS LIES IN ACCEPTING EACH OTHER'S WAYS, NOT WINNING EACH OTHER OVER TO OUR "BETTER WAY" OF DOING THINGS.

Differences enrich marriage the way cultural diversity enriches a community. In our product design and marketing business, we took a less democratic approach and used a standard system of cataloging and storing data. Company files were systematically organized, yet employees organized their personal files however they wanted.

At home Mary Lou files and tracks all important family documents in a carefully arranged cabinet. If I need a document, I ask her for it and give it back to her for filing. I have some basic file folders in my desk, but more for long-term storage than for daily reference. Mary Lou is in and out of her files all day long and is very good at keeping them organized. I rarely refer to my file folders. I am not extremely messy and she is not extremely neat, so our styles don't conflict. Some couples may think about converting partners to their way. In marriage, you must kill the urge to feel "it's my way or the highway."

---

*Develop Your Trust Habit:*

*Today, catch yourself when you want to instruct your partner to do something your way. Instead, tell them you would be glad to help with something if they need it. If they ask how you would do it, show them and ask them to show you if they discover a way that works better for them. This shows you trust their ability to think for themselves.*

---

## Relax and Enjoy the Ride

**Dennis:** One test of understanding and acceptance comes when Mary Lou and I are riding together in the car. When we began dating, I drove and she sat in the passenger seat. Throughout most of our marriage, when we rode together, I felt it was my job to drive. She used a silent language to let me know how I was doing. Whenever

I came to a less than careful stop behind another car or at a red light, she would thrust her right foot out as if she were braking the car herself from the passenger side. Her eyes would widen and she would grab hold of the armrest like she was bringing a horse to a stop from a full gallop. Of course, there was no need to panic. I was in total control.

About ten years ago I learned a new lesson about control. I developed "sensory neuropathy," a condition of deteriorating nerves that affects my feet and makes it painful to keep my foot on the gas. Driving became painful if I had to sit behind the wheel for longer than 30 minutes. Mary Lou gladly took over driving. Now I sit in the passenger seat—where I have learned to trust her driving.

In the beginning, it was hard to keep from thrusting my right foot like Mary Lou did when we approached an intersection. It took awhile, and eventually, I learned to give up control and enjoy the ride. Now she occasionally asks which route she should take, and I say, "You're the driver." When she says, "I know this isn't the fastest way to go, but I like this road," I say, "Great." Mary Lou is a fine driver and I try to be a fine passenger by respecting her driving decisions. Proof of trust and love is often a matter of keeping your mouth shut and showing confidence in your partner. The car is a great place to practice restraint.

*Develop Your Trust Habit:*

*Today, if you are in the habit of backseat driving, hold your tongue. For some, the urge to instruct can be overwhelming. The next time you are in the car together, keep your driving advice to yourself and see if your partner notices. Respectful silence can also be a great trust builder.*

## Why Do You Have to Do That?

A woman is bothered by the fact that her husband taps his tooth-brush on the sink before applying toothpaste. She complains, "Why do you have to do that?" He argues, "Why *don't* you do it?"

Another man takes over control of placing toilet paper on the roller because his wife always mounts the roll with the loose end hanging down against the wall instead of outward facing the toilet.

A wife insists on hanging pictures so the center of the frame is at five feet four inches above the floor—her eye level; her husband insists the bottoms of all the frames should start at forty-six inches above the floor, so they all start at the same level.

Where do we get these ideas about the way things are supposed to be? Maybe it was how a parent did it, or it was done by an actor we respected, or something we read in a magazine. Regardless, imposing our rules on our partners is a recipe for disappointment. Expressing love is about accepting each other's style and silent language.

---

*Develop Your Trust Habit:*

*Today, watch for a little thing your partner does that bothers you, the kind of quirk that makes you want to fix or change them. Then think about the little things you do that seem normal to you, but are different than your partner. Does complaining about them fit into your mission statement for expressing love? Work toward accepting your partner as they are, and they will be more likely to do the same for you.*

---

## Trust, but Verify

When we started our business, a man with many years of business experience told us, "People don't pay their bills." Like the suspicious wife, he believed: "People will cheat you if they can." He advised us not to extend credit, but to make buyers pay cash in advance or cash on delivery.

The standard payment terms in our industry were "Net 30" meaning customers normally paid 30 days after the date of the invoice for goods they received. If we had started our company with the philosophy that customers by their nature would take advantage of us, we would have missed a lot of business. Over thirty years of selling products to thousands of customers, we never had a year in which we wrote off more than 2% of sales to bad accounts, including bankruptcies. In other words, 98% of our customers proved trustworthy. Not that we weren't cautious. We didn't ship products to customers we knew from history or reputation weren't likely to abide by our terms. As former President Ronald Reagan famously said when it came to counting Russia's claim of nuclear missile stockpiles, "Trust, but verify." It is possible to be blinded by infatuation, but we don't need to spend a lot of time with someone before we get a pretty good feeling about whether they are trustworthy—and equally as important, trusting.

*Develop Your Trust Habit:*

*Today, ask yourself if you feel secure in your relationship. When you feel secure you don't think about trust or betrayal or worry your partner will hurt or betray you. If you feel insecure, do something to make your partner feel loved. Positive acts can make you and your partner feel more secure.*

## Consistency Builds Trust

The Coca Cola® brand epitomizes consistency and reliability. Atlanta pharmacist John Pemberton created the Coca-Cola Company in 1886. Pemberton's bookkeeper Frank Robinson coined the brand name and drew the flowing Spencerian script that forms its timeless logo. Since its origin, that logo has remained pretty much the same, while the company has relied on varied advertising forms, slogans and packaging to keep Coke's message current with the times.

When the company tinkered with taste, trying to introduce "New Coke," in 1985, the Atlanta-based corporation felt the wrath of its loyal customers who practically took to the streets in revolt. The company discovered how much their success depended on consistency and brand promise to meet customer expectations.

Companies create new looks in packaging and find fresh advertising slogans that appeal to successive generations, but there had better be an extremely good and obvious reason to fiddle with its underlying character.

Imagine entering a store to make a small purchase and the normally congenial owner asks if that's all you are going to buy today, and says it in a manner suggesting you have a duty to spend more. Maybe you tell yourself he's having a bad day, or he needs the sales this month, so you let it slide. Still, his behavior puts you on edge.

The next time you need something you think twice before returning to his store.  Maybe next time you buy online where you don't need to worry about the owner's attitude. At home when you act sweet and accommodating one day and moody or demanding the next, you can create an atmosphere of unpredictability and mistrust. Your attitude broadcasts you can't be trusted.

## Consistency Makes Room for Spontaneity

Being consistent and predictable may sound boring to someone who likes spontaneity. But consistency doesn't preclude spontaneity. In fact, it can foster an emotional climate that enhances creativity. A chef has to believe that water will boil at the same temperature every day to give him the confidence to create new dishes. We need to know our computers will function if we want to send an email.

> IF OUR COMPANY ISN'T CONSISTENT IN ITS
> MISSION AND MANAGEMENT POLICIES, WE
> WOULDN'T HAVE A BOX TO THINK OUTSIDE OF.

Consistency gives us the confidence to know the sun will be there every day even if we can't see it through the clouds. That's what we want from our partners, to know that they are there for us, especially on stormy days.

## Trusting Each Other's Ways

*Mary Lou:* Trust is about accepting each other's way of doing things. Aside from times when Dennis is helping me get ready for guests, we have our normal household routines. For example, we have different tactics for washing the dishes after a meal. I grew up learning a method used by my father. Even though we had a dishwasher, he learned his technique from his mother before dishwashers were common household appliances.

First, Dad scraped the food off the plates into the garbage can or the disposal. Then he filled the left side of our double sink with hot soapy water and the right side with clean hot water. He washed each plate in the soapy water, rinsed it in the hot water. Then he set it on the counter to be dried.

Dennis learned to wash dishes in a deep, undivided sink, so he cleaned the food off the plate into the garbage can, then scrubbed the plate clean with soap and rinsed it from the faucet, letting the waste-water flow through the drain while using the removable stopper to catch excess food scraps. One of his siblings in the family of five kids dried the dishes by hand.

While Dennis and I never argued about whose way of doing dishes was correct or more efficient, when I do the dishes I clean them my way. When he does dishes he cleans them his way. If we have guests and there are a lot of dirty dishes, we work together, and whoever does the washing decides on the method. The other helps—without questioning the method.

Because of how we learned the process, we both feel that our personal way is, if not better, then definitely more comfortable. That's how we learned and that is how we will do it until we die. To avoid silly arguments over whose way is better, we let each other be ourselves.

*Dennis:* When Mary Lou is preparing a meal for guests and I see she is running behind, I ask if I can pitch in to help her finish. This used to create as many problems as it solved. Why? When she asked me to do something, I would immediately ask, "Why do you want me to do that?" She would then look at me with frustration because she knew that time was running out and our guests were about to arrive. "Will you please just do it? I don't have time to stop and explain."

If I continued questioning the need for the task, she would shake her head, take a deep breath and stare at me with eyes narrowed to slits, a look she perfected while teaching school. "Okay!" I acquiesced, even though I still didn't think the job needed doing. It took a few minor skirmishes for me to realize when I offered to help her, especially when she was up against a deadline, I wasn't helping by questioning her competence or her instructions. I eventually learned to trust that she knows what she is doing and I would help the most by doing what she asks.

*Mary Lou:* I am eternally grateful. His willingness to do the job has made me more open to discussing my plans early enough that he can offer suggestions and improve the plan. That way we are able to prepare everything in advance and have time to entertain our friends together.

## Evasion Destroys Trust

The manufacturer of a leading cholesterol drug used full-page ads in national newspapers claiming their pill "reduces the risk of heart attack by 36%." The tiny print below the headline obscured the facts underlying their claim that read, "In a large clinical study, 3% of patients taking a sugar pill or placebo had a heart attack compared with 2% of patients taking [the company's drug]."

Anyone who read and analyzed the fine print would understand that out of 100 patients in the study, the company's drug helped one person more than those helped by the placebo. The advertising headline claims that 36% of the patients were helped, implying it was more than one patient out of a hundred in the study. Exploiting the subtle difference between "implication" and "inference" is a key tactic used in persuasion. The old saying that "Figures don't lie, but liars figure," is a testimony to how companies manipulate information, especially percentages, to their advantage.

This verbal sleight of hand implies a conclusion without making an outright claim. Advertisers *imply* or suggest relationships, so consumers will *infer* or conclude something is factual, even though the relationship may be irrelevant. The cholesterol drug manufacturer's claim of 36% reduction of risk factors *implies* that the drug reduces heart attacks. In fact, the drug merely reduces levels of LDL cholesterol, not heart attacks. Yet most patients, and even many doctors who prescribe the drug, *infer* that it *does* prevent heart attacks even though there is no proof.

When we want something—whether it is to sell a drug, promote a point of view or make ourselves look better on a resume´—we are tempted to evade. Our language even allows for fudging. Otherwise, we wouldn't say we were being "completely honest" when "honest" would suffice.

Where expediency is valued, misdirection and deceit are apparently acceptable. We even seek permission to evade the inconvenient. Take a group of pedestrians waiting at a red light. Suddenly one steps into the street and crosses. Others trickle out and within seconds virtually everyone is crossing on red. One person's behavior implies it is okay, giving the others permission to cross, regardless of convention. They're doing it, so why not me?

What does this have to do with relationships? Close to home, a husband tells his wife he was late for dinner because he couldn't get away from the office. While it was true he was at the office, he doesn't disclose he was playing poker with his buddies. It's a lie to avoid conflict. He thinks, *no harm no foul.*

Consider the wife who is late for dinner some night. She tells her husband she has to help a friend with some personal issues. She doesn't disclose that the personal issues involve shopping for new shoes together. She thinks *that doesn't seem like a big deal.* Failing to disclose little things to our partners may not seem important. We reason what they don't know won't hurt them. Evasions of the truth, partial disclosures or not telling the whole story may protect us from immediate criticism or complaint, but lies, no matter their size, won't protect us from hurting our own self-esteem.

**PARTNERS MAY NOT KNOW THE TRUTH, BUT IF YOU HAVE A CONSCIENCE YOU WILL LIKELY FEEL BAD ABOUT HIDING THINGS FROM THE PERSON YOU LOVE.**

The film *City Island* is a dramatic example of how secrets, minor and major, can poison family relationships. The minor secret within this movie family is that both parents and both children pretend they don't smoke, yet each one lights up when the others aren't around. The principal character played by Andy Garcia carries a major secret he has kept from his wife for more than 20 years. His concealment clouds their relationship and threatens the marriage. For anyone who has not seen the movie, we won't reveal more, but it is a powerful example of how the fear of disclosure can poison relationships.

## Truth Builds Trust

"You want the truth; you can't handle the truth!" Jack Nicholson's memorable line from, *A Few Good Men*, underscores the belief that our partners can't handle certain knowledge, so we hold information back. Ironically, withholding says we don't trust them. The counter effect is they don't trust us either.

Disclosing our every thought when it's immaterial to our relationship is silly. But withholding information out of fear that our partners are too weak or unpredictable to be trusted would be like a doctor not informing a patient she has cancer because knowing the truth is too painful. Shaping the truth to make it more palatable or to protect our own backsides is a trust buster, not a trust builder.

> TRUSTING EACH OTHER TO BE OPEN AND HONEST IS CRUCIAL TO ACHIEVING INTIMACY AND SUSTAINING LOVE. THERE IS NO ROOM FOR FEAR, REPRISAL OR RECRIMINATION.

## Projection Bias Limits Our Ability to Trust

Why are we so quick to judge and condemn others? One reason is what psychologists call "projection bias," a kind of ego myopia that blindfolds us with our personal self-centered attitudes, interests and opinions. Projection bias is what helps us pick a side on some issue or subject even when we know nothing about it except what we hear from those who support the position.

Media purveyors are adept at delivering programming targeted at our biases. They know we want to see or hear what reinforces our points of view, not what weakens them.

Projection bias, while comforting because it bolsters our beliefs, can seriously hinder our ability to accept or understand our partners. Projection bias might even be considered a form of disability because it limits our ability to feel empathy. Accepting our true loves as they are requires empathy and understanding.

*Dennis:*  I have served on two juries, both regarding criminal cases involving either murder or attempted murder. In both cases, all 12 members of both juries appeared to be reasonable, articulate adults. We all heard the same facts presented by lawyers, yet invariably each member of the jury had a different interpretation of what they heard and saw in the courtroom. One case took days of discussion, listening to each other's viewpoints to reach unanimous agreement.

We all projected our bias about the facts and about the character of the witnesses, the lawyers, even people in the gallery. Some jurors were certain of the defendant's guilt while others were convinced of his innocence. Emotions on each side colored the drama that unfolded in the courtroom and jury room. Bias is never clearer than when 12 men and women sit together to determine someone's fate. One of the more predictable expressions of bias heard in a jury room is, "I know what the defendant was thinking."

### WHEN YOU PRESUME TO KNOW WHAT IS GOING ON INSIDE ANOTHER'S HEAD, YOU CAN BE SURE YOUR BIAS IS WORKING.

Jury service is enlightening. It brings out the bias in everyone and teaches us the need to challenge our own certainty. Defeating our biases makes us better citizens and easier to live with.

In business, projection bias can be comforting but dangerous to the health of a company. No matter how much we think we know about what people want to buy, customers constantly surprise us. Mary Lou and I created more than 50 simple products that reached the market. About 10% were very successful; 10% moderately successful; 60% just paid their way; 10% were dogs not good enough to keep selling, and the final 10% was what we called "dogs with fleas."

In every launch of a new product, however, we were certain or at least very confident we had a winner. It felt great when we predicted correctly and humbling when we didn't. In some cases, we even began to question our judgment, not only about the product's potential but our capacity to think clearly. Inventing new products requires a lot of confidence, but when bias got in the way we usually failed.

Companies build trust and loyalty in their brands by listening to their customers and finding ways to satisfy their real needs. We build trust and loyalty with each other by doing the same.

**BIAS IS DANGEROUS TO YOUR RELATIONSHIP BECAUSE IT MASKS YOUR ABILITY TO CORRECTLY UNDERSTAND YOUR PARTNER'S OPINIONS, IDEAS, DREAMS AND DESIRES.**

## Show 'Em You Know 'Em

Shopping for gifts is difficult when we don't know the recipient well. Even when we do, it's too easy to pick gifts that appeal to us instead of them. We often miss the obvious because we are too sure when we like something, others will too. Staying in love, however, is not about satisfying yourself. It's about satisfying your customer. Showing your partner you know them well builds trust. Doing something that confirms you don't know them builds walls.

The esteemed cartoonist, Charles Schulz, creator of the comic strip *Peanuts,* once had Charlie Brown give his friend Lucy a pocket-knife for her birthday. Of course, the inappropriate gift was shrewd of Charlie, who hoped Lucy would see little need for the knife and would simply give it back to him. Schulz had a keen grasp of human nature, especially when pointing out no one is more interested in us than ourselves.

## Paying Attention Builds Trust

We went to a party one night and ran into a guy we hadn't seen in months. We immediately noticed something different about him. We didn't recognize what had changed until he told us he'd shaved off the mustache he'd worn for years.

We all transform over time and are often oblivious to those changes in others and in ourselves. Companies lose customers because they ignore changing trends and tastes. It's easy to take others' needs for granted and miss subtle transformations.

How many times has a woman put on a new dress or worn her hair differently, or a man cleaned the windows or trimmed the hedges and heard no comment from their partner? Noticing changes and commenting on them builds trust. It tells our partners we appreciate them.

### As in business, relationships are subject to the laws of competition.

If we fail to treat each other well, challengers are standing by making it easy for our true loves to leave. The marriage contract is a promise to love each other for life, but it doesn't amount to a guarantee.

Marriage weaves together our monetary assets and liabilities, but it doesn't guarantee our partner's affections. We earn love and trust by how we treat each other.

## WE BUILD TRUST BY BEING CONSISTENT. WE LOSE TRUST BY SHAVING THE TRUTH.

We build trust by accepting and respecting our partners' unique qualities. We build trust by revealing our own strengths and weaknesses, and by showing that we know our partners well and are paying attention to the changes in their lives.

## Have Faith in Each Other

*Mary Lou:* Understanding and accepting our differences isn't limited to cultures separated by national borders. Relationships between men and women of any culture, or the same culture, are subject to an endless number of misunderstandings and struggles for control of physical or psychological territory.

Dirty tricks may be the order of the day in politics but not in business partnerships or marriage. Unlike politics, marriage requires absolute trust in each other's motives. Married couples can't be looking for reasons to feel hurt, criticized, ridiculed or victimized.

## LOVE AND TRUST MEAN GIVING EACH OTHER THE BENEFIT OF THE DOUBT.

Early in our marriage, Dennis told me that no matter what conflict we had, no matter what I might say that could be interpreted as negative, he trusted it was never meant to hurt him.

By trusting me, I trusted him. That promise of faith in each other is the real proof of love we all seek. It is what allows us to work through disagreements and to trust we have each other's interests at heart.

Below are five Habit Focus questions for this chapter to help you assess your Habit of Trust. The purpose of these questions is to make you think about your own level of care, not your partner's care.

Each of you can use a separate sheet of paper to record your assessments. Then come together and share your results. A nine rating means you "agree" with the statement. A rating of one means you "disagree." Use your answers to start a conversation about your perceptions and expectations. Remember this is about giving your partner the kind of customer care they need.

# Habit Focus 8. TRUST

1. I show confidence in my partner.

| 1 | 2 | 3 | 4 | 5 | 6 | 7 | 8 | 9 |
|---|---|---|---|---|---|---|---|---|

2. I respect my partner's personal style.

| 1 | 2 | 3 | 4 | 5 | 6 | 7 | 8 | 9 |
|---|---|---|---|---|---|---|---|---|

3. I have proven myself to be trustworthy.

| 1 | 2 | 3 | 4 | 5 | 6 | 7 | 8 | 9 |
|---|---|---|---|---|---|---|---|---|

4. I am not a backseat driver.

| 1 | 2 | 3 | 4 | 5 | 6 | 7 | 8 | 9 |
|---|---|---|---|---|---|---|---|---|

5. I am never evasive with my partner.

| 1 | 2 | 3 | 4 | 5 | 6 | 7 | 8 | 9 |
|---|---|---|---|---|---|---|---|---|

# 9. ROMANCE

Australian actor Hugh Jackman, aka Logan, was once designated *People Magazine*'s "Sexiest Man Alive." When he appeared on TV on the *Ellen De Generes Show*, Ellen asked him what his wife considered sexy. He answered, "Taking out the garbage."

Surveys show that women looking for marriage partners seek men who offer enduring love and security, who share their view of the world and who deeply understand them. What makes them feel loved is "romance." But, a recent survey of what married women consider romantic may surprise most men because it often has little to do with sex. Some of their answers were:

- Helping around the house without me asking

- Talking with me and giving me his complete attention

- Inviting me on a date and taking care of all the details

- Buying me fresh flowers once in a while

- Going for walks and holding my hand

- Touching me for no reason

- Writing me little notes that say he loves me

No single definition of romance is going to fit everyone. If we asked high school or college-aged women what they found sexy or romantic in a man, the answers would vary from those given by a married woman with children. A woman who loves to dance might place "good dancer" at the top of her sexy man list. Other women might list a man's physique, his smile, his earning power, his sense of humor or his confidence.

Men surveyed about what they find sexy in a woman, mention physical attractiveness, intelligence, and a warm smile. In 2016, college-aged men mentioned a woman's earning power.

Surveys may point us in a general direction of what large numbers of people are thinking, but surveys can be misleading. Knowing what most people think about sex and romance isn't very helpful to any specific person or couple.

## THE ONLY SURVEY OPINIONS THAT SHOULD GUIDE US ARE THE ONES HELD BY THE PARTNER SHARING OUR BED, OUR BANK ACCOUNT AND OUR CHILDREN.

On average, men have ten times more testosterone in their blood than women, That makes them generally more aggressive and interested in sex, but each individual's level of testosterone can vary dramatically, influencing their interest in everything from sex to sports to poetry. Studies done by Dr. Helen Fisher and others at Rutgers University, and published by the Society for Neuroscience, looked at the chemical reactions in the brains of men and women in the early stages of their relationship. They located areas in the brains of these subjects showing high levels of dopamine, a brain chemical that produces feelings of satisfaction and pleasure. Elevated dopamine levels are linked to increased energy, motivation to win rewards and feeling euphoric. The more romantic the research subjects said they were feeling during the tests, the more elevated their dopamine levels.

There was a difference between the men and the women tested. Most of the women showed more activity in the areas of the brain linked to reward, emotion and attention. Most of the men showed activity in visual processing areas, including one associated with sexual arousal.

## WHO WE ARE IS AFFECTED BY THE MOLECULES IN OUR MINDS, BUT OUR BEHAVIOR IS THE BEST EVIDENCE OF WHO WE ARE WITH OUR LOVE MATE.

Until we become customers of each other and understand and care about each other's unique needs, romantic and otherwise, we will never be able to stay in love any more than a business will be able to hold on to its customers. No question, the business side of living together—satisfying kids' needs, overcoming a bad day at the job, longing to escape from daily pressures—all put a damper on romance. A larger problem is how differently partners feel about sex and romance. Traditional social scripts go back centuries and play a role in shaping our expectations.

## Romance Is Passionate Care

In 1850 the renowned poet Elizabeth Barrett Browning published a book of poems titled *Sonnets from the Portuguese*. Perhaps the best-known poem in the collection is "How Do I Love Thee Let Me

Count The Ways," written for her husband and fellow poet Robert Browning. Only fourteen lines long, her opening words show the intensity of her love. "I love thee to the depth and breadth and height my soul can reach..."

Consider replacing one word in the title of Browning's exquisite sonnet to read, "How Do I Love Thee Let Me *Show* The Ways." Writing a love poem is a fine way of showing feelings, but for the poetically challenged, how many other ways can we show our love?

Dozens of books have been written listing things we can do for each other, but lifting an idea that someone else thinks is romantic won't necessarily work for everyone.

## TO SHOW YOUR LOVE IN MEANINGFUL WAYS YOU HAVE TO KNOW WHAT YOUR PARTNER DESIRES AND NEEDS.

Women say romance is not only a symbol of affection, it is a deeply felt, joyful pleasure that arouses their passion and feelings of love and loyalty. Just as Vitamin C boosts immunity from the common cold, romance builds intimacy and lasting love. Romance is testimony to a woman that she matters to her husband. It's proof of his love and its deficiency makes her feel unattractive, angry, anxious and resentful. When romance fades in marriage, she begins to wonder if the attention and care she received from him while they were dating was just a walk down the proverbial garden path to get what he really wanted: a cook, a maid and regular sex partner. Ironically, whatever he expected from marriage, especially sex, is lost to him because of her discontent. It is pretty clear to men that romancing a woman can open the door to sex, but it isn't always clear to him that his own needs are more likely to be met when he gives her what she needs.

A man struggling in an unhappy marriage may understand, theoretically, that romance is important, but when it is missing, he doesn't

get muscle cramps like he would if his body were deficient in elec-
trolytes. He doesn't get a physical sensation telling him something is
lacking. In contrast, lack of romance does ring bells in a woman. She
feels the loss of romance in an elemental way.

## If Romance Were Measured Like Cholesterol

*Dennis:* If only romance had a number like cholesterol, and we
could measure its benefit to our hearts through a blood test. If we
felt our hearts were in danger of a stroke we would get right with the
romance program.

> IF ROMANCE COULD BE TIED TO A PURCHASE
> ORDER OR ITS VALUE MEASURED BY PRICE TO
> EARNINGS RATIO, MEN WOULD FIND A WAY
> TO GROW IT, HARVEST IT AND SELL IT FOR A
> PREMIUM PRICE.

In business, when a deal capturing a major new account is consum-
mated, the successful salesperson knows customer care (romance) is
essential to keeping the account. To ensure a long-term relationship
he sends thank-you notes, birthday cards and emails asking about
the customer's children and inquiries about their favorite hobby.

We communicate in whatever way we can think of, without
becoming a pest, to keep ourselves and our company uppermost in
the customer's mind. Most importantly, we listen with rapt attention
like a detective unraveling the clues to a mystery. Ironically, we often
forget how to use our investigative powers at home. After signing the
biggest deal of our lives, the marriage contract, we often neglect to
take care of the most important customer we will ever have. Maybe
the motivation to care is as simple as receiving a payoff such as a
purchase order resulting from a successful sales campaign. At home,
we might take our true loves for granted because we don't connect

our daily behavior to a specific goal—expressing our love. At home, men don't have a money reward driving their actions. Not everyone is a salesman with the goal of making a sale, but the point is, most men are at their best when they have a goal, a measurable purpose or a tangible problem to solve.

### WHEN A WOMAN WONDERS WHAT HAPPENED TO THE ROMANCE IN HER RELATIONSHIP, SHE THINKS HER PARTNER DOESN'T WANT HER.

When a salesman's best customer hints that she is thinking about opening her account for review, it means she is looking for a new supplier. That's when she starts shopping elsewhere and is flooded with renewed attention. An unhappy wife is like a dissatisfied buyer of goods and services. She may consider changing vendors when she feels that her business has been taken for granted.

Men may feel their role in marriage is to be a protector and provider, not romancer. Men don't need to be told how to defend their homes or families. That's instinctive. Romance is not. If a man held the title of Chief Romance Officer, he might take his mission of providing romance more seriously. This is why many men need a reason or a protocol to be romantic. If they haven't been assigned a specific area of responsibility, or don't perceive an immediate threat, they may assume that all is well. They may not be romantic unless it can be connected to important events such as anniversaries, birthdays or other significant dates with etiquette stipulating what is expected of them.

## Romance Is More Than Foreplay

*Mary Lou:* Flowering plants use their color and movement to attract bees. Plants need bees to ensure pollination. A woman may use her appearance to attract a man, but just as a man with money may want to be loved for himself, not his wealth, a woman may want to be valued for her core spirit, her soul.

When a woman seeks a permanent partner, romance without sex is one kind of proof that she has found her soulmate, the person who will hold her hand and walk with her, listen to her dreams and care about her—far from the bedroom.

Some men believe that romance is merely foreplay leading to sex— otherwise it's not required. Of course, romance may lead to sex, but when romance feels like a trade for sex, she may feel his romance is designed to help himself not her. A woman, of course, can be primarily interested in sex, too, but that woman probably doesn't complain about what romance might lead to.

A woman who does complain, needs romance to confirm she is desired for her very essence, not for a man's gratification. When she does feel the romance is for her, she will care more deeply about giving back in many other ways. When she feels loved, she is more able to reciprocate love.

## Romance Is About Keeping the Customer

Given the divorce rate of about 1.2 million couples per year in the United States, it seems that many couples are oblivious to their partners' romantic needs. However, romance must have been alive and well at some point or they would not have made it to the altar. That makes us believe that we use romance to achieve our goal of getting the customer, but simply don't understand its value when it comes to keeping the customer. During courtship, when hormones are operating on overdrive, men may be more romantic, or may just appear to be romantic to a woman wearing her own love blinders.

When the mating dance is done and the rose-colored glasses come off, romance requires conscious effort. We don't call that work, we call it marketing. This is where knowledge of romance, and even romance training, would come in handy. Marriage becomes a struggle for men with no formal training in how to act romantically with women who expect romance.

*Mary Lou:* Dennis and I had been married for about five months when the *Superman* movie featuring Christopher Reeve opened. I was excited about seeing it and curious about this new actor. When we got to the theater and found a parking place, Dennis asked me to wait a minute before we got out of the car. Then he reached behind my seat and brought out a single red rose. Of course, I was surprised and delighted and I asked him what was the occasion. He said, "It's not easy competing with Superman."

I have never forgotten that moment. Dennis never fails to give me flowers on special occasions, but he also surprises me with bouquets when I least expect them. He says it is just to let me know that I am on his mind. Those little gestures make me want to do more to make him happy.

## Learning About Romance

Even within emotionally starved families, girls can still read or hear stories about fairy tale princes and princesses. On the other hand, boys have no clear romantic models. They grow up playing action heroes, learning about protecting the planet from alien invaders and saving maidens in distress. They rarely learn scripts that favor romance. Talking among buddies about romance is a threat to the masculine persona, which is about sexual prowess.

Romance does not come naturally to many men and is sorely lacking in their education and play. Some men may emulate romantic behavior they see in their fathers or in films or on television and act in romantic ways during courtship. But if romantic effort doesn't continue in marriage, their partners are left feeling confused and rejected. The inability of men to embrace romance makes women all the more suspicious that men's romantic acts are associated with conquest and not directed at them in particular. This makes tangible proof of love even more essential to a woman.

A woman may seduce a man by playing to his fantasies of sexual conquest or his dream of a happy home and children, but the romantic icons she desires, such as flowers, aren't typically satisfying to a man. She can gush with delight upon receiving roses, but it is still difficult for a man to feel the depth of her pleasure from flowers.

If a woman is more verbal than her husband, she will feel romance when he invests time just talking with her, touching her hand and giving her his undivided attention. He may not feel the same kind of pleasure. He may need to consciously think about how to be romantic and plan for it, whereas she might feel more spontaneously romantic.

Romantic effort is also important to a woman. He may use flowers, jewelry, picnics in the park or surprise vacations to demonstrate his love. But few men understand that all gifts feel more romantic to her if they required considerable effort on his part to acquire.

## Romantic Signals

Libido is defined as sexual desire and the energy to have sex. It's affected by age, health, stress, hormone levels and many other factors including the complications of daily living. Romance, too, influences libido. "The relationship between what happens in the genitals and how people feel about it is more complex than we realized," says Erik Jansen, a research scientist at the Kinsey Institute at Indiana University in Bloomington. "You can feel desire without showing any signs of physical arousal, and you can have physical arousal without showing signs of desire." This complicates our romantic signals. One woman explains how hard it is to know how to respond to her husband when she doesn't know what he wants.

"I have just gotten the kids to bed and finished a load of laundry and I still have some paperwork to take care of from the office, and he comes up behind me and starts kissing me on the neck and rubbing my back. At this point, I am not in the mood. I'm tired, plus I'm angry with him for not helping me with dinner and the kids. When I don't respond to him, he gets upset and wants to know what's wrong. I tell him that I am not in the mood. He says he just thought I needed a hug. He walks away and we don't talk to each other the rest of the night. I feel like a bitch because I thought he wanted to have sex."

It is easy to get your signals crossed when your romantic and your sexual needs are out of sync with your partner's. A common language would help communicate your romantic aims, as would a heightened awareness of how your partner is feeling at particular moments. Clear signals communicate what you have in mind, but like seasoned poker players, you also have to recognize your partner's "tells." For those who don't play poker, a "tell" is a quirk, habit, or idiosyncrasy that gives away our hidden intent.

Tells are subconscious expressions outside of our awareness. For example, if you are holding a good hand of cards, you might unconsciously convey your excitement with a twitch of the eye. Players who are aware of their own tells often wear dark glasses to keep competitors from reading their eyes. Successful players strive to purge their play of behavior patterns that expose their emotions. But staying in love requires the exact opposite kind of agenda.

### In Marriage, unlike in poker, concealment is a losing hand.

Romantic signals are complicated. They have to be clear, but not so direct they feel demanding or could invite rejection. Men grow up learning to, "say what you mean and mean what you say." When it comes to love and romance, however, straight talk is not the brand of foreplay that appeals to many women.

## SEX AND ROMANCE TASTE SWEETER WITH A BIT OF MYSTERY STIRRED IN AND SERVED WARM VIA SUGGESTION AND PROMISE.

You go through a stage early in the relationship when you are ready to rip each other's clothes off at the drop of "hello," but when the dopamine dwindles, spontaneity suffers. Individually, you know when you feel like making love, but knowing when your partner is in the mood is not always clear.

Remember when you first fell in love but were afraid to be the first one to mention the "L" word for fear of rejection? A version of the rejection game lingers years into marriage. You want to feel the romance, but don't want to sound like you are ordering a burger or closing a business deal. When your partner wants to have sex and you don't, for whatever reason, things get even more complicated. This is where romantic signals come into play.

If poker is a game of eliminating signals, baseball is the opposite, overflowing with signals. Baseball couldn't exist without hand signals that communicate between the manager in the dugout to the base coach, from base coach to base runner and from catcher to pitcher. A base coach may use a complex series of movements such as a touch of his cap, his left ear, his left hand over his right forearm and a couple more motions combined to tell the batter whether to bunt, hit away or take the next pitch.

Imagine the comedy if we developed a set of baseball-like love signals to announce our romantic intentions. Obviously, this can get silly in a hurry. Still, signals can communicate intent in those odd moments when words aren't possible or feel clumsy.

We all have romantic gestures such as "the wink," the knowing smile, the sensuous back rub or the subtle rise of an eyebrow and a nod toward the bedroom. We rely on our own special communiqués but it's easy to get signals crossed when we either don't know what the signals mean, they aren't consistent or we aren't paying attention.

So let's have some fun with crazy signals starting with "semaphores," the flags used to transmit information from aircraft carriers to pilots landing their planes. They could be used to get a partner's attention by making an "XXX" with the flags. Or we could mount a standard roadside "Yield" sign on the bedroom door. Olympic Pictograms might work, such as the one representing "Greco-Roman wrestling". A little "Help Wanted" placard could always be propped up on a pillow. The red and yellow penalty cards used by soccer officials could be adapted by changing the meaning of the colors.

How about directional graphics? A large arrow set on the floor and pointing into the bedroom could be a good hint. Maybe you could even find an amusement park sign, representing your favorite ride, and drag it out when you were in the mood for some real fun. Get the idea? This doesn't need to be serious. Signals can be fun, though we are not necessarily recommending any of the above. Just think of them as icebreakers to jump-start your discussion.

Every signal needs a response to ensure the message is received, understood and answered. Emails or text messages are always good for announcing your intent, especially if you create a unique style of invitation just between the two of you. The hard part is when you get the invite but aren't in the mood. It's essential that you tell your partner you love them, but need a rain check because you have too much cluttering your brain, or you are nervous about something or not feeling well.

WHATEVER WAYS YOU DEVISE TO SEND
ROMANTIC SIGNALS, IT IS VITAL THAT YOU
ALSO AGREE ON A WAY TO SAY, "NOT RIGHT
NOW" AND BE OKAY WITH IT.

*Develop Your Romance Habit:*

*Today, conduct your own survey about what your partner likes and dislikes by playing, "Would You Rather." Here's how it works. Ask you partner random questions that offer an either/or choice such as: • Would you rather I give you a back rub or a foot rub? • Would you rather spend 30 minutes talking together or take 30 minutes of quiet for yourself? • Would you rather have only social media or TV to watch for the rest of your life? These questions can be as carefree or as deep as you wish to learn more about your true love's thoughts and feelings. The purpose of the survey is to discover more about each other.*

## Why Men Don't Read Romance Novels

For men, romance invokes idealized adventure, excitement and the potential for heroic achievement, all to win the fair maiden's approval. Romance novels, however, tell a different story about why romance appeals to women—both today and centuries ago. Debora B. Schwartz, Associate Professor of English at California Polytechnic, teaches the origins of romance literature. She says that in the 12th century, stories about romance started to be written down in what was called "French vernacular," to distinguish it from "real" literature written in Latin. The audience for these early romantic tales was mostly women, including the queen and her ladies of the court. They wanted stories about women in the central roles, rather than epic tales of male conquests as was common in stories such as Beowulf.

Romance literature is filled with tales that women want to hear about the quests that men would endure for love. They need evidence that the quest for adventure is not what drives the man. The pain he is willing to endure is motivated by his love for her. To be assured his love is real and eternal she needs ongoing proof. Romance is one verification.

According to the Romance Writers of America (RWA), the romance genre is now the largest fiction category in publishing, comprising about 25% of all novels printed. In 2016, there were 18 writers listed in the Romance Writers Hall of Fame. None of them were men. That gives us a good idea of the role romance plays in women's lives, and conversely how little it fits for men, who don't care or know enough to even write about the subject.

## Romance Without Sex

The popularity of Author Stephenie Meyer's *Twilight* series is an affirmation of how early in a girl's life romance can captivate her imagination. At the height of its popularity, the *Twilight* series novels occupied four of the top five spots in *USA Today*'s list of best-selling books. Meyer's heroine is a teenager named Isabella Swan who falls in love with a vampire named Edward Cullen.

The stories show how seductive romance, sans sex, can be for a young girl. Isabella and Edward are unconditionally and irrevocably in love though they (in the early books) had merely kissed a few times. In his past, Edward has only fed on the blood of animals, but he now craves Isabella's with a starving passion.

This primal desire for each other powers the romance. For Bella, simply speaking Edward's name is a thrill all its own. Edward is rendered nearly helpless by Bella's scent, which he describes as like freesia. The romantic tension captured the hearts of young women worldwide. With all of its success, however, the books failed to interest a young male audience, though young women say that boys should try reading about Edward and Bella to learn what girls really find romantic.

As research in the next section regarding brain research describes, boys' brains are wired differently from girls' brains. As a result, most boys don't read much, and when they do, it isn't about romance. Romance charms the interests of young girls, but most boys prefer action and gore or the latest search and destroy video game or live competitive sports.

A boy's interest in ghoulish adventure is a disadvantage for men when it comes to knowing how a woman wants her romance served. Women writers create the brand of heroes that fulfill female desires, making these novels the perfect road map for romance. Few real-life men read these books, however, so they miss the clues about what women need and fantasize about.

How many times have we read a story or watched a film in which the cool new European character comes to town only to dazzle the local females with his wit, charm and attention to their needs? The plot succeeds because it feels true. The stereotypical young American male is portrayed as a ball of confusion trying to understand women.

## So What Do Men Need?

Dr. Louann Brizendine, the author of *The Female Brain,* said that when she mentioned the idea of writing *The Male Brain* to colleagues, she received an almost universally humorous response: any treatise on the male brain would no doubt be very short—maybe even just a pamphlet.

The doctor took her subject more seriously, though, finding that men are far more complex and interesting than many women think. Maybe because men are designed more for action, for defense and for constructing the bridges, roads and buildings we take for granted, we think of them as less sensitive, maybe even less in need of romance. For men, romance is about challenge, achievement, recognition and respect.

Women want to be swept up in the arms of heroes, and men want to be those heroes. Young men are driven by libido, nature's imperative to procreate. Men's brain scans show they think about sex every ten seconds. A lot of their thinking processes are inherently driven by massive amounts (compared to women) of testosterone, which is also what drives men to construct, conquer and control the world around them.

Men learn to first please their mothers, then their girlfriends and ultimately their wives and daughters by achieving success. By proving their strength, prowess and skill at navigating an ever more complex and dangerous world, they earn the esteem and admiration of the women they love.

Men are told in many ways that whatever path they choose in life, failure is not an option. It is the scent of failure that men hate and women fear in men; it disrupts the natural order of his achievement and therefore her reward. Men want to be loved no less than women want to be loved, but men feel loved in different ways. Sex with the woman he loves is evidence of her desire for him and her endorsement of his expertise, his competence and his mastery.

• Romance for a man is the look in his lover's eyes that makes him feel admired—for his strength, intelligence, integrity, his ideas or whatever he deems valuable.

• Romance is laughing at his jokes.

- Romance is the smell of fresh-baked bread.

- Romance is public approval of his talents, skills and success.

- Romance lies in her physical attractiveness on display at his side.

- Romance is in the meals she prepares and the care she takes making his home feel welcome and comfortable.

- Romance is sharing his interests in sports, business, the outdoors or whatever hobbies and pastimes he enjoys and wants her to enjoy with him. Talking with a woman feels romantic for her, and sharing activities is more likely to feel romantic for him.

These ideas of what is romantic are of course generalities. They give hints, but don't describe each unique customer. Ultimately, your partner is the only one who can define their romantic needs. When they do, you must pay attention. They may not always voice their needs, but great marketers are more interested in what people *do* than what they say. Observing their behavior can lead you in the right direction.

I

When money is tight, and you resist spending on anything but necessities, keep in mind that romance is not about spending money. It's more often about spending time and finding creative solutions that demonstrate thoughtfulness.

When a man says he needs a new putter to improve his golf game, you don't need to point out that he already has four putters leaning up against the wall in the garage. Most men have heard the old maxim that it's not the arrow but the archer that makes the difference. Wanting a new putter may be a way of saying he isn't happy with his performance, and he doesn't know what to do about it so he blames it on his equipment. Your discussion doesn't need to be about putters. It needs to be about his state of mind. By probing his feelings about golf and what he thinks about when he plays, you give him a chance to share his feelings. Maybe he lacks focus because he feels guilty about the amount of time he spends playing golf. Maybe other golfers don't want to play with him and he feels rejected. Maybe he's just not athletic and will never get any better at the game.

> REGARDLESS OF THE REASONS FOR HIS STRUGGLE, ROMANCE IS ABOUT LISTENING TO HIM, SHOWING INTEREST IN HIM, HELPING HIM EXPRESS HIS ANXIETIES. IT'S NOT ABOUT TALKING HIM INTO OR OUT OF A NEW PUTTER.

When men want to talk about their feelings or need to solve a problem, they often say they need a "sounding board." In other words, they need you to hear what they are thinking. Romance, for both men and women, means listening without judgment.

Substituting the word *care* for romance or sex gives the word new meaning. Romancing the customer with care and attention works in business to keep them coming back. Romance also works miracles at home. It makes us feel loved.

## Romance Is Being Interesting

Companies grow and prosper when they continually increase benefits to their customers. We sold ten different products to QVC, the TV shopping channel. Some items were short-lived and were presented on-air only a half dozen times, while others lasted several years. Customers stayed interested in products we continuously improved. Every few months the QVC merchandise managers and category buyers pushed us to add something new to our presentations, so customers would feel we were consistently exceeding their expectations. We were committed to creating new products, and as a result, we rarely had trouble getting appointments to see buyers at the major retailers who are hungry for new products, the adrenaline of business. Likewise, new experience is the adrenaline of marriage.

We have all spent time in restaurants watching a couple dining in silence at another table. They look like they have been together for years, yet they seem to have nothing to say to each other. How can that be? How can people run out of things to talk about? The world doesn't stop spinning when we start living together. Just as a good business devotes resources to research and development in order to remain competitive, you must bring something new to the table each day if you are going to stay connected and engaged. Love can feel as comfortable as an old shoe, and you don't need to be chattering away every minute you're together. However, when marriage loses its energy, like when a company's products have lost their sparkle, it's a warning sign you need to increase investment in your relationship.

## A GREAT BENEFIT OF MARRIAGE IS GETTING A FRONT ROW SEAT TO ONE ANOTHER'S PERFORMANCE.

*Dennis:* Mary Lou and I have been together for more than 40 years, and every day we try to add something new to engage each other. One benefit of marriage is keeping each other interested in life. I can talk about what interests me, but being *interesting* is more about finding things to interest my only customer. For example, Mary Lou loves to knit. When she starts a fresh project, like knitting a tiny sweater with a hood for her cousin's newborn boy, I am curious about what it will look like and how she goes about seamlessly joining the hood to the sweater body. I am "engaged" in her interests. I look forward to the outcome and watching her excitement when she sends it off to her cousin. I get to take part in the satisfaction she feels from a job well done when she gets an email photo of the baby wearing her creation. The benefits we enjoy through each other's care are essential to staying in love. The old benefits are no less important than the new ones that revitalize our energy.

Book publishers maintain what they call a "backlist" comprised of previously published works still worthy of staying in print, even though they aren't as sought after as new titles. A great backlist is essential to the overall health of the company. In marriage, you have a backlist of benefits that you may take for granted, like having one of you "bring home the bacon" while the other one cooks and serves it.

## Appreciation Is Romance

The things you do for each other contribute to romance and to staying in love. You can make a difference by promoting each other's efforts through recognition and appreciation, much the way employees are recognized for their contributions to a company's success. It's not hard to say:

- "Thank you for a fabulous dinner."

- "Thank you for managing our finances."

- "Thank you for getting the kids ready for school."

- "Thank you for making the bed every day."

- "I love your kisses and the way you touch me.

*Dennis:* In our company, Mary Lou created a Crunch Award, a framed document designed by Fred Palmer, our amazing graphic designer. It was awarded to an employee who helped another employee during a stressful time when they really needed help to meet a deadline. The worker who benefited from the assistance nominated the one who helped out and the whole company participated in an awards ceremony recognizing the effort. The recipient received an actual oversized Crunch Bar® to sweeten the award. Crunch time at home is fairly common, too, and it doesn't hurt to make a big deal out of it when your partner pitches in to help you out.

## Encouragement Is Romance

Another of the great benefits you can provide each other is unwavering support, cheerleading and confidence-building. These are especially valuable when times are tough. Critics claim that marriage partners shouldn't need to be praised or constantly thanked for doing the expected. They say taking out the garbage or cleaning the house is routine business, and applause should be reserved for exceptional achievement.

> WITHHOLDING APPROVAL OR APPRECIATION MAY INCREASE THE FEELING OF CONTROL ENJOYED BY THE CRITIC, BUT A STINGY SPIRIT CRUSHES LOVE.

*Dennis:* I played basketball in college and then three or more days a week until my late fifties. When a teammate scored a basket, we applauded him. When he made a mistake, we still encouraged him. Encouragement lifts the spirit. When you give, you get in return, creating a powerful bond of mutual support and trust. Camaraderie is one of the benefits of team sports, and it is even more important in marriage because it's a team that can last a lifetime. Cheering each other promotes the team spirit necessary to solve life's puzzles and survive its setbacks.

In their classic business book, *The One Minute Manager,* authors Ken Blanchard and Spencer Johnson advise managers to "catch an employee doing something right" and praise them for it. Another way to be romantic and stay in love is to catch your partner doing something well and make them feel good about it. That shows you are paying attention and care about them. To understand the most important benefits you receive from your true love, try to imagine which ones you would have a hard time living without.

We all need someone to listen to our tales of glory, no matter how ordinary. It is a gift we would miss if no one was there to hear us. We want a partner to comfort us when life beats us down. We yearn for a partner who is generous with their time, empathizes with our worries and celebrates our achievements. We need someone lovable to love us. We need someone thoughtful to think of us. We need someone caring to care for us. These are the true benefits that help us stay in love.

## Habit Focus 9. ROMANCE

1. I am romantic and I show it to my partner.

| 1 | 2 | 3 | 4 | 5 | 6 | 7 | 8 | 9 |
|---|---|---|---|---|---|---|---|---|

2. I spend time talking with my partner.

| 1 | 2 | 3 | 4 | 5 | 6 | 7 | 8 | 9 |
|---|---|---|---|---|---|---|---|---|

3. I support my partner's hobbies and interests.

| 1 | 2 | 3 | 4 | 5 | 6 | 7 | 8 | 9 |
|---|---|---|---|---|---|---|---|---|

4. I give my partner clear romantic signals.

| 1 | 2 | 3 | 4 | 5 | 6 | 7 | 8 | 9 |
|---|---|---|---|---|---|---|---|---|

5. I give my partner great pleasure.

| 1 | 2 | 3 | 4 | 5 | 6 | 7 | 8 | 9 |
|---|---|---|---|---|---|---|---|---|

# 10. Personal Care

If you devote so much time to giving your partner great customer care, you may worry you won't have time left for yourself. Still, you must take care of yourself if you're going to be physically and emotionally healthy enough to care for others. This chapter is about how to give yourself the passionate customer care you need.

## First, Be Prepared to Care for Yourself

When you fly commercially, before takeoff a flight attendant always announces, "In case of an emergency put on your oxygen mask first before you assist other passengers." The same holds true for passionate care in marriage. You need to take care of yourself first to be able to care for your partner.

In marriage, as in most things in life, you are responsible for your own health and happiness. Your partner can lighten your load and create opportunities for you to succeed, but only you can choose how to think, act and feel at any given moment. According to research done by Dr. Sonja Lyubomirsky and published in her 2008 book *The How of Happiness,* you can increase your happiness through your intentional actions. Here are what we call intentional actions.

## Three Parts of You That Need Care

Caring for yourself is not about pampering or taking spa days—although those are delightful if you can afford them and have the time. Caring for yourself is not about taking separate vacations, either—unless it's something you and your partner enjoy. Caring for yourself is about digging deeper with a focus on these three parts of your being: your mind, your heart and your body.

- **Part 1. Mind Care** is about maintaining a positive mental outlook, listening to your intuition, being mindful and decisive.

- **Part 2. Heart Care** focuses on the emotional, empathetic and intuitive part of your being.

- **Part 3. Body Care** attends to your physical health and fitness.

# Part 1. Mind Care

Life is about choice. We can choose to be positive or negative. We can choose to be satisfied or dissatisfied. We can choose to stay or leave a marriage. We can choose to forgive someone or hold a grudge. A healthy mind is better equipped to make healthy choices. So how do we develop a healthy mind?

You've probably heard the saying "garbage in, garbage out." It originally referred to computers. If you enter flawed data, you'll end up with flawed conclusions. Your mind is no different. If you feed it garbage, it won't serve you well. On the other hand, be positive and be honest with yourself and nourish your mind. This includes clarifying your decision-making process. The more equipped you are to examine problems, the less confusing and stressful they'll feel. Become a better decision-maker and you'll find it easier to cope with the complex problems that affect you individually and as a couple.

## Four Steps to Clarifying Your Choices

Making decisions, especially when we must choose among only painful alternatives can be frustrating. Objectivity is difficult when emotions swirl inside us. Sometimes, we make choices based on what we impulsively desire without analyzing potential outcomes. Here is a four-step method we find useful in making decisions, especially important and complex ones.

**Step 1. Preparation.** In the chapter on Preparing to Care, we talked about how preparing to care for Mary Lou's mother made it easier to satisfy her needs. When you are prepared, you can calmly handle surprises. If you anticipate that things can go wrong, you'll be ready to pivot.

> MENTALLY PREPARING YOURSELF TO BE HIT WITH UFOS, THOSE UNEXPECTED FRIGGIN' OBSTACLES, IS HALF THE BATTLE IN LIFE.

Likewise, when you are mentally prepared to make choices, you won't always act on impulse. If it's a big decision, take time to consider how your choice will affect you today and in the long term. Prepare yourself by gathering information. Make a list of pros and cons to examine the impact on your physical, social and financial life. Don't be in a rush to make decisions you haven't taken time to think about.

**Step 2. Evaluation.** Next, evaluate the information you gathered in Step 1. Analyze your desires and separate them from objective data. If you want to buy a car, for example, your right brain may want the upgraded sound system at only ten more dollars a month. Then your left brain reminds you that over the 48-month term of the loan it's actually \$480. Is the cost worth it? Where else could you use that money?

## EVALUATION IS OFTEN A MATTER OF MAKING TRADE-OFFS. ASK YOURSELF WHAT OUTCOMES YOU EXPECT OR WISH TO ACHIEVE FROM YOUR DECISIONS.

For important problems and questions, use the list of pros and cons you gathered in Step 1. Write them down side by side on a piece of paper, so you can review them more than once and picture them in your mind. Part of the evaluation process is also getting other people's opinions. Share the list with your partner and friends you trust and ask for their thoughts. When we designed the cover for this book, we posted different designs on Facebook and asked friends to choose which one they liked best, rather than relying exclusively on our own tastes.

**Step 3. Decision.** After you've evaluated a problem, give yourself a deadline to make a decision. In choosing this book cover, we gave ourselves three days. That way we wouldn't hold up the printing and publication. If you still feel comfortable with your decision after it's made, you can feel confident it's the correct one. On the other hand, if you continue to fret about it or argue with yourself after making a decision, don't be afraid to change it. Part of feeling comfortable with our book cover design was the 90% positive responses we received from others. Before asking friends to help, we had originally created a completely different cover design. After we let it sit for a few months, it didn't feel right, so we sought help from our friends. You're not a politician, so don't fear being branded a flip-flopper when you change your mind.

## SOMETIMES AN INTERNAL CONFLICT REVEALS SOMETHING YOU DIDN'T CONSIDER IN YOUR PREPARATION.

For example, we changed the original yellow background for the book cover design after reading that blue book covers appeal to both men and women. So we tested the yellow and the blue covers. Blue was preferred about ten to one over yellow. Then we tested different titles and *Five Star Love* won. Our friends told us what appealed to them and we listened. Not all life choices can be turned into market research, but objective input will give you a different perspective and help you make better decisions.

Some decisions involve selecting from two bad alternatives, also known as a "double bind" or getting trapped "between a rock and a hard place." When you feel trapped, take a deep breath and pick the best of the bad alternatives and move on. Procrastination won't solve the problem and it can make you doubt yourself and eat away at your confidence. Don't let a painful situation stop you from making a choice and moving on. Even if it turns out to be the wrong choice, most mistakes can be fixed with new information.

**Step 4. Action.** Finally, act on the decision (unless your decision is to do nothing after completing the steps above). If you decide you're going to improve your mind by studying economics so you can understand how the Federal Reserve banking system works, do it. If you always wanted to learn another language, do it. The enemy of choice is fear. It can paralyze you from making a decision. You may not be able to avoid fear, but you can certainly conquer it. Once we made our final book cover decision, we sent the design to the printer and didn't turn back. That was not a monumental problem, but most decisions we face in life aren't. We still need to make them.

In her first section of *Big Magic, Creative Living Beyond Fear*, author Elizabeth Gilbert talks about dealing with fear. In her brilliant metaphor, she describes going on a road trip knowing Fear will come along because it always does. She stipulates that she will be driving the car on this road trip with Creativity sitting shotgun, and only she and Creativity make the decisions. Fear stays in the back seat, and it never, ever gets to drive.

> ## CARING FOR YOUR MIND MEANS EXERCISING IT. IF YOU DON'T TAKE ACTION, YOU'LL BE STUCK IN THE PRESENT.

## Intuition Is Also Useful in Making Decisions

Have you ever used a coin toss to make a quick decision? When the coin is in the air, and you're hoping for a certain outcome, you know you've already made your choice, so go ahead with it. If you really don't care, you'll be happy to follow whatever the coin decides.

When facing a big decision such as what house to buy or what job to take or where to raise your children, it's wise to include your intuition in the decision. Dr. Hendrie Weisinger in a 2015 article "Intuitive Decision Making" in *Psychology Today* lists these tips for using your intuition in the decision-making process.

- When you look in a mirror or talk to someone else about this decision, what do your facial expressions and the sound of your voice say about how you feel? Are you hesitant and fearful or confident and excited? What does your body language say?

- Have you taken action to show you are committed to your choice? How are you moving forward? What do you see in the year ahead when you consider the impact of this decision?

*Mary Lou:* Here's an example of including intuition in your decision-making. At one point in our marriage, when our business was booming, we bought a large lot on a golf course in Castle Pines, Colorado and planned to build a dream home/office there. Throughout the planning process, my gut kept telling me that moving was a bad decision. I didn't say anything to Dennis because he was so excited about the design. He lit up when he talked about it, and he described it so beautifully that I had mixed feelings.

Even though the new home would be grand and we could add all the features we'd dreamed of, I couldn't get rid of this voice inside that kept telling me something wasn't right. I kept my thoughts to myself because I hoped I would eventually fall in love with the project. I told myself the fear of change was holding me back.

When our French distributor for several of our products came for a visit, we took him to the site and showed him the plans. He looked puzzled and said, "Why would you give up your priceless view of the mountains in your current house for this one you can find on almost any golf course?"

His comment gave me a flash of insight. I realized I didn't really share Dennis' vision of living on a golf course. After combining my intuitive feelings with the projections of the cost and the risk to our business if sales dropped, I told Dennis what I was feeling. He listened and we decided to stay where we were.

### WHEN MAKING DECISIONS, IT'S CRITICAL TO SCRUTINIZE YOUR OWN IDEAS AND FEELINGS SO YOU CAN CLEARLY COMMUNICATE THEM TO YOUR PARTNER.

The time to lay everything out is at the beginning before too much time and money have been invested. Trust, respect, communication and empathy are all important. You must represent yourself effectively so your true love knows what is in your mind and heart. Your goal is to combine your ideas to create something new for both of you. Mind Care is about maintaining a positive mental outlook, listening to your intuition and being mindful and decisive.

## Maintain a Positive Mind

A 2002 Yale University study showed that people with a positive outlook live seven years longer than pessimists. It concluded that positive thinking is even more important than lower blood pressure and lower cholesterol levels. Imagine adding seven years to your life just by your mental outlook! If you don't like your story, you have a choice to rewrite your script to become the person you want to be. It starts with choosing to be positive and taking responsibility for your life and your desires.

*Mary Lou:* I have learned it's important to pay attention to the stories I tell myself, especially the negative ones. Keeping my mind open and joyous leads to a life of smiles.

I'll admit, for example, that sometimes I might feel frustrated with Dennis about something, even though I haven't told him exactly what it is. Then, if he doesn't fulfill my expectations I feel let down. Let me use cleaning my car as an example. I often wish Dennis would clean my car for me because I'm too busy. I tell myself, "Can't he see how dirty the floor mats are? Can't he see how dirty the windshield is just by looking at it? Doesn't he care about me driving a dirty car?"

Now, I could go to a good friend and complain that Dennis should clean the car because I don't have time. I could go to great lengths describing how thoughtless he is. But that doesn't clean my car, and now I've dumped my frustration at my friend's doorstep and possibly ruined her mood. Blaming my frustration on him because I don't have time to do something may help me express my disappointment for a moment or two, but experience tells me that complaining won't make me feel better and could cause a needless argument. Instead, I've learned to look at the other side and be an advocate for him and tell myself his side of the story. I think, he's just as busy as I am, plus he's not a clean freak about the car, so he may not feel the car needs cleaning. If it's so important to me, I should take the time and get the job done myself. I can drive to a car wash or get up early one morning and do it myself at home.

Digging deeper, I realized something even more important was influencing my decision. My dad used to keep my mom's car clean, and I subconsciously wanted Dennis to do the same for me. Once I understood the emotional undertone involved, I understood my feelings and realized why I was making my dirty car his problem.

By going through this whole crazy dialogue in my head, the complaint runs out of steam. I can let it go instead of throwing it at the man I love. I can keep my positive feelings going instead of ruining my day and his. I tell the negative chattering monkeys inside my head to sit down and shut up. If the dirty car continues to nag at me, then I can discuss it with Dennis at one of our Stop-Start-Continue meetings.

**TAKING CARE OF YOUR MIND MEANS CHAL-LENGING YOUR THOUGHTS AND DESIRES TO GET A THREE-DIMENSIONAL VIEW OF YOUR WORLD INSTEAD OF RELYING ON WHAT'S GOING ON IN YOUR SELF-CENTERED HEAD.**

When you take responsibility for your desires and needs instead of making your partner responsible for fulfilling them, you get a clearer picture of who you are, and that leads to a healthier mind.

## Clear Your Mind of Old Wounds

Another important part of taking care of your mind is making sure the stories you tell yourself aren't continually opening old wounds. How often do you or your partner start discussing something, and before you realize it, you are in a heated argument because you brought past hurts into the present discussion? Instead of focusing on the current issue, now there is a truckload of emotional dynamite in the room. It is so important to forgive one another and let the past go. Exiling painful baggage will clear your head and allow you to be in the moment.

---

*Develop Your Personal Habit:*

*Today, you can remove an old wound from your past. Write a letter that pours out the hurt you're feeling; then burn it and watch the pain turn to ashes. Write "I forgive you!" on a slip of paper and insert into a balloon, then blow it up and watch your worry float away. Put items that symbolize the pain into a box and bury it somewhere.*

---

## Calming Your Mind Is Caring for Yourself

The wonderful thing about being human is you get to choose how you think and feel. Becoming more "mindful" will also help you get there. Attention to mindfulness has risen as we look for a way to calm ourselves in our fast-paced, media-based culture. We think of mindfulness as "focused awareness."

Imagine this chaotic scene. You are in the Grand Central Terminal in New York City. All around you bodies are in motion, rushing in every direction. The multiple arrival/departure boards seem to be changing by the second. People are pointing and panicking. Body odors swirl around you. Confusion reigns. It's your first time in the great hall. Your heart races. You feel lost and anxious you will miss your train if you can't find the right departure platform.

Now close your eyes, relax your body and focus on your breathing. Breathe in slowly and breathe out. Visualize the air as a soothing cloud. Draw it into your lungs and then out into the surrounding space. Let your mind float above your body and see yourself as a lighthouse in the storm. The chaos is reduced to a blur. Gradually, your heart resumes its natural rhythm and you feel calm. When you open your eyes, you feel prepared to focus your awareness on the present moment. You'll find your train. Everything will be okay.

## CALMING YOUR MIND IS A POWERFUL WAY TO CARE FOR YOURSELF.

If your thoughts wander and you're unable to focus or reach conclusions about actions you need to take, it can make you feel less than capable. Your inability to control outcomes can make life feel unfair and confusing. A calm mind puts you back in control and can boost your confidence.

Here is another scenario. Imagine that tonight you're preparing a dinner for ten people. They're about to arrive and a ton of things still need to be done. This is a moment made for making you feel inadequate. You have a choice. You can feel like a volcano about to erupt...or...you can take a deep breath, relax and tell yourself what gets done will get done. Your friends care about you. They don't require you to be perfect. And if something doesn't get done, that's okay, because friends are more likely to empathize with your flaws than your perfections.

Imagine you are launching a first-time webinar to sell your new book and your internet service goes down just as you are about to deliver your bonus offer. Imagine you are making a presentation in front of the board of directors and your laptop freezes. Imagine you are driving on the freeway and someone in a massive truck is tailgating you but you can't change lanes because you're boxed in by another truck. Life is filled with these anxious moments that raise blood pressure and make us want to scream, pound the table or throw something against the wall, or worse—lash out at the people we love.

Being mindful is not the same as being thoughtful. Thoughtfulness is about managing your outer self and your actions toward others. Mindfulness is about managing your inner self and your thoughts.

Being mindful helps you stay in the moment so you can manage distractions and disappointments. The more often you practice the easier it becomes. Find time each day to be present in your life, if only for ten minutes at a time.

Throw out all the mental garbage and negative thoughts you've collected in your life. That will help you be present for yourself and your partner. Let go of regrets. Focus on a positive present. That will free your mind. Feed your mind healthy thoughts and experiences and you'll attract more of them in return.

---

*Develop Your Personal Habit:*

*Today, do something to practice mindfulness. You aren't required to sit in the lotus position to be mindful or meditate. You can lie on the bed and relax for ten minutes and just listen to your breathing. Go for a walk and clear your mind by focusing on your feet as you walk. Take a drive on a less traveled street or highway and pay attention to the sights and sounds. Just observe and enjoy.*

---

# Part 2. Heart Care: Your BE–Attitudes

What does it mean to take care of your heart? We're not talking about your physical heart, although of course, that is important. We aren't referring to your emotions, either. You can care for those by becoming more mindful. The "heart" we're talking about is your essence, your spirit, your virtuous self, your values.

CARING FOR YOUR HEART IS ABOUT
PRACTICING THE VIRTUES YOU ADMIRE IN
GOOD PEOPLE, SO YOU BECOME THE HERO IN
YOUR OWN STORY, THE PERSON YOU WANT
TO BE, THE PERSON YOU ADMIRE.

So how do you get to this virtuous place? Caring about something means giving it your time and attention. What virtues make you an admirable person? A good place to start is by giving your attention to what we call *The Seven Be-attitudes of the Heart.* They are

1. Authenticity

2. Empathy

3. Courage

4. Faith

5. Gratitude

6. Hope

7. Patience

Caring for your heart means living these seven virtues. Let's take a closer look at each one.

## Be Authentic

What does it mean to be authentic? One way to define a word is to examine its opposite. The opposite of authentic is fake. It's easy to describe what it feels like to be a fake. It's called guilt. But what feeling accompanies authenticity? Jesus told his apostles, "The truth will set you free," so, if living a lie makes us feel guilty, perhaps we can say that living the truth, being authentic, makes us feel free and motivates us to be honest with ourselves—and our partner.

You've probably heard the saying, "Fake it till you make it." The purpose of that advice may be to encourage us to face each quest in life with confidence even if we don't feel it in the beginning. Faking confidence, however, is not the same as being a fake. It's essential to believe you can do something even if you've never done it before. Here's an example.

*Dennis:* When I was studying to be an architect, I applied for a job with an architect in my hometown of twelve thousand people. His first question to me was a test, "Can you survey a piece of property for me?" The property in question was a small pocket park in the center of town. He needed to know the lay of the land so he could design a structure on the property. I didn't know at the time how I would complete his challenge but I was confident I could figure it out. I was faking it before making it, and overcoming my fear of failure.

First I went to the library, checked out a book on surveying and read it. The next day I went to the local city engineer's office and asked to borrow the survey equipment I needed. They obliged, one of the benefits of living in a small town. I enlisted my brother-in-law Frank to hold the survey pole while I operated the transit. Thanks, Frank.

I used the information we gathered to plot the property elevation lines on a large sheet of architectural vellum and returned to the architect's office a few days later and presented him the rolled-up drawing. He opened a plan drawer showing layers of drawings. To my surprise, there lay another drawing with the park's title hand-lettered on the side. I felt my face flush as he unrolled my comparatively crude drawing and spread it out over the top of the existing park survey. He examined my elevation lines to see if my drawing resembled his professionally done survey. He studied it for a minute or so, then he looked at me and said, "Close enough." He hired me to work four hours a day for the entire summer. One of the problems with being human is the fear of not being good enough. We lie about little things just to feel we are more than we believe we are. Each lie we tell ourselves and others is a scar on our heart.

**BEING AUTHENTIC IS ABOUT ACCEPTING YOURSELF AS YOU ARE, BELIEVING YOU CAN RISE TO THE OCCASION IF THE CHALLENGE DEMANDS IT. THE BETTER PERSON YOU BECOME, THE BETTER PARTNER YOU WILL BE.**

## Be Empathetic

Some say the only way to feel truly empathetic is to have experienced exactly what someone else is experiencing. When you think about it, that's impossible. A man, after all, can't feel like a woman, or a woman like a man. A cop can't feel like a judge. A Catholic priest can't feel what the father of a child feels. One parent can't know precisely what another parent is feeling about a child with cancer because every parent and child are different, and every moment in time is different. Accepting that reality, however, shouldn't stop us from caring about what someone else is feeling. Empathy is the essence of caring for others. The more we care, the closer we come to feeling empathy.

Why is empathy important? Because without it, no one matters. If no one matters, that includes us. It follows, therefore, that if we want to live in a world that does matter, we must find ways to feel empathy for others.

By showing someone that we care about their experience, we bring them closer. We also grow by adding their experience to our own. That increases our awareness and capacity to feel empathy for people who are different from us. Awareness reduces our fear and anxiety and opens us to even more new experiences. Even if we can never be truly empathetic, seeking empathy makes us more caring for others.

## Be Courageous

Courage comes in many forms. Courage can be taking an unpopular political position. It can be standing up against injustice. It can be writing something while knowing you'll be severely criticized. Helping others in dangerous moments can build courage. Courage is also about getting up and going to work every day when you hate your job but love the family that depends on you. Courage is committing to learn a skill that won't help you today, but hopefully will in the future. Courage is taking a chance on love. We can be inspired by stories of heroism and choose to act courageously when the need arises.

### THE TEST OF COURAGE LIES IN THE WILLINGNESS TO TAKE ON A CHALLENGE WITHOUT A GUARANTEE OF SUCCESS.

Sometimes courage is saying, "I refuse to live like this anymore." Henry David Thoreau wrote, "The mass of men lead lives of quiet desperation." What he may have meant was this: as we strive to acquire more things, we can never get enough. We are caught in a never-ending cycle of wanting more and never finding satisfaction with what we have. Courage can be ending the cycle of desire and accepting ourselves for who we are and what we have.

### SOMETIMES COURAGE IS SAYING NO TO MORE.

In caring for ourselves we must have the courage to look inside our hearts and question who we are. And if we don't like what we find, have the courage to change.

## Be Faithful

Your faith is based on your belief in yourself and where you fit in the universe. Faith is your answer to, "Why do I exist?" It's the worth you place on yourself, and it gives you the confidence to go out into the world and strive to do what you think is right.  Your faith forms the attitudes you have about how to treat others. It guides you in your sense of right and wrong and helps you connect with others who hold similar beliefs. It gives your life a sense of purpose and shapes how you view death and what might come after death. It's something only you can decide for yourself.

### THE ESSENCE OF FAITH IS LOVE AND FORGIVENESS.

No one is perfect. When we make mistakes, our faith in the future motivates us to learn from our mistakes and move forward determined to be better. Your spiritual life is a constant striving to be a better person, to do good and to recognize the good in others.

## Be Grateful

Gratitude creates a rich heart. It keeps us open to our partner, to our children, to our family, to our friends and co-workers, to new people we meet and to our surroundings. We didn't have the opportunity to pick our parents or where we were born. That's luck. We do have a choice, however, when it comes to celebrating every day and finding ways to fill our hearts with joy.

### A HEART FILLED WITH GRATITUDE CLOSES THE DOOR TO DESPAIR AND OPENS THE DOORS TO HOPE AND LOVE.

Sometimes in our bleakest moments, we focus on the bad and forget to see joy. We forget that when one door closes, another one opens—if we let it.  By searching for ways to be grateful, even in our darkest days, we let hope in. Gratitude deepen friendships. Think about the kind of person you want to spend time with. Are they full of complaints, grief and dissatisfaction or acceptance, joy and contentment?

Are you a friend to yourself? Do you show yourself appreciation and support? Being grateful for what you have, instead of comparing yourself with others, will reduce feelings of envy that also give rise to guilt. Practicing gratitude in your marriage will also strengthen your relationship because your partner will feel appreciated and cared for.

---

*Develop Your Personal Habit:*

*Today, track the number of positive and negative expressions you make in your daily routine. How many expressions of gratitude vs. criticism fill your day? How often do you compliment others, including your partner? How often do you show appreciation, support and encouragement versus how often do you express cynicism, sarcasm, or show disapproval? Decide where to improve and take action.*

---

*Mary Lou:* When I met Dennis I was 25, and I had already given up on marriage. I decided I would just date and focus on my teaching and that would be enough. I was tired of meeting men who were only concerned about their power and wealth. They didn't know much about sharing or caring. Then I met Dennis—in a bar—and my life changed forever. I was filled with gratitude to meet someone who really understood me and loved me the way I am.

When we married, I got a two-for-one deal because Dennis already had a son. Even though I yearned to have children of my own, it didn't happen for us. Teaching gave me a new opportunity each year to have between 25 and 35 students to nurture and watch grow. If it weren't for Dennis, Jr., I wouldn't be a parent and feel that incredible love that exists between a parent and a child. I'm so grateful for both of them. The door to having children closed for us, but a new one opened and delivered a son to me. Now thanks to our son and his beautiful wife, we have a granddaughter who is kind and thoughtful and smart and brave.

## FIND WHAT YOU APPRECIATE IN YOUR LIFE AND KEEP A GRATITUDE JOURNAL TO PRACTICE YOUR APPRECIATION SKILLS.

You can make lists or write about special moments that you can use later to remind you of the good things in your life. The more you notice the beautiful gifts in life, the more your heart fills with joy. A smile is something free you can give away every day.

## Be Hopeful

If you think about your favorite superhero, you see someone who is in the business of hope. Let's take Superman. Clark Kent is just an ordinary guy but when all appears to be lost he can change into a superhero, fighting for all that's good and right. Why do we respond so viscerally to superheroes? They represent hope. They help us fight the desperation that comes with hard times.

*Mary Lou:* In the recession of the early 1980's we lost our income, and we lost our first home in foreclosure. When a notice went up on our front door, I wanted to hide in the basement and never go out again. I was devastated and felt like a failure. It was even worse when I went into the teacher's lounge at my school and one of the teachers announced in a loud voice that he noticed the foreclosure listing in the morning paper. Mortified, I left the lounge and headed to the bathroom for a good cry.

My embarrassment and sense of failure overwhelmed the physical loss of the house. I still had to face those teachers every day, and

I still had to go home at night and pack. I had a choice to make. I could spend time feeling sorry for myself and blaming the people and circumstances that got us to this point, or I could look to the future and hope that things were going to get better. I could look down for the rest of my life or I could look forward and get back up. I chose hope because I wanted a better future. I knew that I had to lift myself out of the deep hole of defeat and deal with moving and finding a new place to live that we could afford.

## IF YOU DO NOTHING, YOU HAVE NO HOPE OF MAKING YOUR LIFE BETTER. BY TAKING ACTION, YOU OVERCOME FEELINGS OF PARALYSIS AND DESPAIR.

We sold one of our cars, and we found a condo that worked with our budget. Dennis started a new business with two partners and made it profitable within a year. I continued to teach to contribute to our income, and I quit worrying about what other teachers thought of me.

The psychologist Charles R. Snyder links hope to goals combined with a realistic plan to reach those goals. He claimed there are three main things that make up hopeful thinking: 1. Approaching life in a goal-oriented way; 2. Finding different ways to achieve your goals; 3. Believing you can cause change and achieve your goals. Hope was the positive force that got me out of bed. Dennis drove me to work every day and picked me up, and we had some of our best conversations during those rides. We were in this together and we were making it work through our hope and our actions. When Dennis and his partners sold the new business, we immediately paid the bank the money they lost in the foreclosure to clear our credit. Over a period of five years, we turned our financial life completely around.

## HOPE DOESN'T LIVE IN A VACUUM. HOPE IS NOT WISHING FOR SOMETHING TO HAPPEN AND THEN DOING NOTHING ABOUT IT.

I had to take care of my feelings and figure out a way to deal with despair. I had to choose to come up with a new future, and then take action to bring it to fruition.

### HOPE IS THE FUEL OF DREAMS AND WORK IS THE ENGINE.

## Be Patient

Do you live on Planet Instantaneous surrounded by your electronic devices and believe you must respond to every request within seconds? Do you react with impatience and even anger when things seem too slow? The demands of our electronic devices have altered how we interact with one another and can impact the most when we are at home with our partners.

When we spend our daily energy supply on listening to others, running errands, and taking care of our partners and children, it's natural that we want a little time for ourselves at night. We want "me" time. Time in the Man Cave or She Cave, reading a book, playing video games or streaming movies. The question is, how can we take care of our own needs and still be patient with all of the other demands on our time?

*Mary Lou:* One way to develop patience is to allow time for life events to unfold. Here's an example. When I show someone an item I've knitted, they usually say, "How long did it take you to make that?" It's as if knitting is a race and speed is the measure of competency. For me, knitting is a hobby that suspends time and allows my creation to build at a pleasurable pace. My patience is tested when I must rip out mistakes and fix them. I used to fume as I unraveled the stitches. Dennis knew to stay away at those frantic moments. Over time, however, I learned that "ripping out" is part of knitting. The process requires acceptance and patience. Time is the enemy of knitting, so when I sit down with my needles and let the garment grow at its own pace I feel like I'm suspending time and learning patience.

I remember one of my favorite quotes from Joyce Meyer. She says, "Patience is not the ability to wait, but how you behave while you're waiting." Here are some techniques you can practice to develop patience while waiting.

- Let events unfold by forcing yourself to slow down. Move and speak more slowly. Imagine you're underwater and feel the weight of the water slowing your arms and legs.

- Wait at least five seconds before replying to a request (instead of the typical 1.5 ) and count to five so your brain engages before your mouth speaks.

- Give someone else a chance to give a thoughtful answer by waiting at least five seconds for their reply.

- Pay attention to your body in stressful situations. Are you breathing faster? Is your stomach tight? Are you sweating? Are your hands clenched? Deep breathing and relaxing your muscles can help you relieve these feelings. Try to view the situation as though you are an eye-witness watching the event without judgment.

- Reflect back to find what triggered your anger or frustration. Understanding how it starts can help you decide how to handle it differently the next time a specific trigger arises. By calming yourself outwardly you can calm yourself inwardly.

- Listen to the internal dialogue you tell yourself when you face a stressful situation. Are you elevating the fact your partner neglected to take out the garbage or cook dinner as proof they are thoughtless and don't love you anymore? Accept that it's just a case of forgotten garbage, not lost love. If the story won't go away, bring it up at your next Start-Stop-Continue meeting with your partner.

• Monitor external factors such as temperature, time of day and how hungry or tired you are. Physical factors can lower your patience level. Monitor your energy levels. If you know you're going to miss a meal, carry a snack with you to manage your blood-sugar level. Allow more time to arrive at appointments when you know traffic will be heavy.

• Don't believe you can change other people. Instead, examine your own behavior and accept others, especially your partner, for who they are.

• Be patient with daily aggravations so they don't escalate into anger and undermine your relationship. Ask yourself whether you'd rather be patient or live alone.

Practice your Be-Attitudes and you have a great chance of feeling positive about yourself and being a better partner, neighbor, friend, co-worker, parent and family member.

# Part 3. Body Care

Your body is your permanent home on earth. How you care for it governs how you feel in it. There are two good reasons to take care of your body. First, you'll feel physically stronger and have more energy to manage daily life. Second, you'll feel more attractive and be more appealing to your partner. Body care is not about looking like a magazine model, it's about respecting yourself.

## Don't Feel Like a Trade-in

Remember when you bought your first new car? It was like owning a little piece of heaven. You couldn't wait to show it off to your friends. The first year, you regularly washed and waxed your beauty. You kept the floor mats clean and fresh. You made sure your windows were crystal clear and the leather pampered. Your car couldn't look or run any better—that first year or two.

Then things began to change. You missed a scheduled maintenance. The car started smelling like the french fries that fell under the seat. The windshield became clouded. You switched from high-octane gas to regular. The waxing fell by the wayside and you subjected your new car to the coarse brushes and harsh detergent at the convenience-store car wash. Your glove compartment filled up with junk. The dog shed hair between the seats and it clogged the air ducts so you could hardly breathe. One morning you looked at your once beautiful car sitting in the driveway and wondered what happened. That little piece of heaven had fallen to earth and looked ready to be traded in on a new model.

The moral of the story is: If you don't take care of yourself, you also may look and feel like a trade-in.

We all know that great-looking cars attract attention regardless of their age. Maintaining your body and mind in a healthy condition will help you feel good about yourself and keep you attractive and desirable to your partner. When you show you respect yourself, others will respect you and be attracted to you.

## OUR FEATURES WILL CHANGE AS TIME PASSES, BUT NEGLECT, NOT AGE, IS THE VILLAIN.

*Dennis:* A young man once asked me if staying in love is harder as you get older. He said, "I don't know if I will still be attracted to my girlfriend when she goets old and doesn't look like she does now." I smiled when I heard this, not because it was funny, rather because it was something I wondered myself when I was about his age. I heard a young woman express a similar fear that her boyfriend would someday morph into his pot-bellied father. She wasn't sure she could live with that.

I wanted to tell my young friend that when you love someone, looks don't matter, but I knew that wasn't reality. Looks are often the first level of attraction. That doesn't mean we need to win a beauty contest. What each of us finds attractive in a partner is intensely personal and inexplicable.

When I first saw Mary Lou, I had no idea what kind of a person she would turn out to be. I was simply attracted to her appearance. From a distance I could see how she walked, the color of her hair, her clothes and her shape, all of which excited me. I wasn't thinking about how she might look in 40 years. I was too excited by what I saw in the moment of discovery.

You may have had a similar experience. You spot someone in a restaurant or at a party and feel an attraction. But, what is it about them that makes you stay in love for life? What is that special something that carries you beyond feeling butterflies in the stomach to sustainable love? It's a combination of their whole being: their mind, their heart and their body. Caring for our bodies is about managing what we can change and accepting change thrust upon us by sickness or accident.

Our bodies change over time for all sorts of reasons including giving birth, aging, illness, depression and gravity. That's why it's so important to remain healthy while we can. Eating nutritious food, exercising and getting enough sleep are within our control and vitally important. When we created new products, we knew a beautiful package would attract attention. But we also learned that customer buying decisions are based more on the product's benefits than its features. Product features appeal to our senses and entice us, but it's the benefits that give us lasting satisfaction.

When we published greeting cards and graphics, one of our marketing maxims was "design attracts; message sells." Buyers are drawn to the image on the cover of a card, but the message inside must also be right to motivate the purchase. We may like the outside, but until the inside is right, we keep searching. Romantic connection is similar. We have to be attracted to the person's form and be satisfied with their substance before we are likely to find a lasting relationship.

> ### WE ALL FIND DIFFERENT FEATURES ATTRACTIVE AND WANT DIFFERENT BENEFITS. THE FORMULA FOR LASTING LOVE IS FINDING THE RIGHT MATCH FOR BOTH.

The young man who asked if it is possible to stay in love as we age may worry about how his true love will look in the future. However, if you treat each other like customers you never want to lose, you won't have to worry because caring for yourself and caring for the one you love will make you attractive for life.

How well are you prepared to care for yourself? On the next page are your final five Habit Focus questions to help you assess your Habit of Personal Care. The purpose of these questions is to make you think about how well you care for yourself.

## Habit Focus 10. PERSONAL CARE

1. I work at staying healthy and physically fit.

| 1 | 2 | 3 | 4 | 5 | 6 | 7 | 8 | 9 |
|---|---|---|---|---|---|---|---|---|

2. I feel empathy for people's problems.

| 1 | 2 | 3 | 4 | 5 | 6 | 7 | 8 | 9 |
|---|---|---|---|---|---|---|---|---|

3. I show I am a patient person.

| 1 | 2 | 3 | 4 | 5 | 6 | 7 | 8 | 9 |
|---|---|---|---|---|---|---|---|---|

4. I feel hopeful.

| 1 | 2 | 3 | 4 | 5 | 6 | 7 | 8 | 9 |

5. I find it easy to calm myself in stressful situations.

| 1 | 2 | 3 | 4 | 5 | 6 | 7 | 8 | 9 |

# Congratulations!

You made it all the way through The Ten Habits of Passionate Customer Care. We hope you see how they can shape your happiness and satisfaction with your marriage right now and for years to come. It is our deepest wish that you stay in love forever, and we hope that this book helps you realize that goal.

Finishing *Five Star Love* is not an ending—for you or for us. Our mission is to build a community of couples who support one another, and we want to hear your story. We would love knowing what worked and didn't work as you tried the different ideas in *Five Star Love*. Our purpose is to give you the notes for creating your own symphony, and music is meant to be played and heard.

Look for another one of our books on Amazon. It's called *The Marriage Story*, a narrative poem about a fictional couple chasing their American Dream. It shows how easy it is for couples to become distracted and distant, losing the love that brought them together. The loss of a job and onset of depression threaten to destroy their marriage. Their challenge is to find their way back to the love they once knew. This touching story is a reminder of how easily love can slip away when we forget what really matters in our lives.

Now it's your turn. We'd love to hear how *FIVE STAR LOVE* and *THE MARRIAGE STORY* have touched your life and your marriage.

Please contact us on our website DennisAndMaryLou.com

# THE MARRIAGE STORY

## A TIMELESS TALE ABOUT STAYING IN LOVE FOR LIFE

DENNIS EDWARD GREEN

# Recommended Reading

Adair, John and Thomas, Neil. *John Adair's 100 Greatest Ideas for Effective Leadership and Management*. Oxford: Capstone Publishing, 2002.

Adams, Barney. *The Wow Factor*. New York: Skyhorse Publishing, 2008.

Adams, Susan. *The Marital Compatibility Test*. Omaha: Adicus Books, Inc., 2000.

Amato, Paul R., Booth, Alan, Johnson, David R., and Rogers, Stacy J. *Alone Together, How Marriage in America is Changing*. Cambridge: Harvard University Press, 2007.

Anderson, Mac. *212° Service: The 10 Rules for Creating a Service Culture*. Naperville: Simple Truths, LLC., 2011.

Anderson, Mac. *Customer Love: Great Stories About Great Service*. Naperville: Simple Truths, LLC., 2008.

Anderson, Mac and Murphy, John J. *Habits Die Hard: 10 Steps to Building Successful Habits*. Naperville: Simple Truths, LLC., 2008.

Arden, Paul. *It's Not How Good You Are, It's How Good You Want To Be*. New York: Phaidon Press, Inc. 2003.

Assaraf, John. *Having It All, Achieving Your Life's Goals and Dreams*. New York: Atria Books, 2007.

Bacal, Robert. *Perfect Phrases for Customer Service.* New York: McGraw-Hill, 2005.

Bhargava, Rohit. *Personality Not Included: Why Companies Lose Their Authenticity and How Great Brands Get It Back.* New York: McGraw-Hill, 2008.

Barry, Dave. *David Barry's Complete Guide to Guys.* New York: Random House, 1995.

Beckwith, Harry. *Selling the Invisible.* New York: Warner Books, 1997.

Beckwith, Harry. *What Clients Love.* New York: Warner Books, 2003.

Benton, D.A. *How to Think Like a CEO; The 22 Vital Traits You Need to Be the Person at the Top.* New York: Warner Books, 1996.

Blanchard, Ken and Glanz, Barbara. *The Simple Truths of Service.* Naperville: Simple Truths, LLC, 2005.

Bloom, Linda and Bloom, Charlie. *101 Things I Wish I Knew When I Got Married.* Novato: New World Library, 2004.

Bowman, Alisa. *Project Happily Ever After.* Philadelphia: Running Press Books, 2010.

Britten, Rhonda. *Fearless Living.* New York: Perigree/Penguin Putnam, 2001.

Brizendine, Louann. *The Female Brain.* New York: Broadway Books, 2006.

Brizendine, Louann. *The Male Brain.* New York: Three Rivers Press/Random House, Inc., 2010.

Byrne, Rhonda. *The Secret.* New York: Atria Books, 2006.

Canfield, Jack et al. *Chicken Soup for the Entrepreneur's Soul.* Deerfield Beach: Health Communications, Inc., 2006.

Chapman, Gary. *The Five Love Languages.* Chicago: Northfield Publishing, 2004.

Cherlin, Andrew J. *The Marriage-Go-Round*. New York: Alfred A. Knopf, 2009.

Cline, Foster and Fay, Jim. *Parenting with Love & Logic*. Colorado Springs: Pinon Press, 2006.

Coleman, Paul. *The 30 Secrets of Happily Married Couples*. Avon: Adams Media, 2006.

Collins, James C. and Porras, Jerry I. *Built to Last*. New York: HarperCollins Publishers, 1994.

Coontz, Stephanie. *Marriage, a History: How Love Conquered Marriage*. New York: Penguin Books, 2005.

Cottrell, David. *Monday Morning Leadership*. Dallas: CornerStone Leadership Institute, 2002.

Daley, Kevin and Wolfe, Emmett. *Socratic Selling: How to Ask the Questions that Get the Sale*. New York: McGraw-Hill, 1996.

Denning, Stephen. *The Leader's Guide to Storytelling*. San Francisco: Jossey-Bass, 2005.

DiJulius III, John R. *Secret Service: Hidden Systems that Deliver Unforgettable Customer Service*. New York: AMACOM, 2003.

DiJulius III, John R. *What's the Secret?* Hoboken: John Wiley & Sons, 2008.

Eggerichs, Emerson. *Cracking the Communication Code*. Nashville: Integrity Publishers, 2007.

Eggerichs, Emerson. *Love & Respect*. Nashville: Thomas Nelson, 2004.

Finch, Lloyd C. *Telephone Courtesy & Customer Service*. Menlo Park: Crisp Learning, 2000.

Fisk, Jim and Barron, Robert. *The Official MBA Handbook of Great Business Quotations*. New York: Simon & Schuster, Inc., 1984.

Ford, Arielle and Zammit, Claire. *The Art of Love Relationship Series*. San Rafael: Evolving Wisdom, 2011.

Ford, Arielle. *The Soulmate Secret.* New York: HarperCollins, 2009.

Ford, Arielle. *Wabi Sabi Love: The Ancient Art of Finding Perfect Love in Imperfect Relationships.* New York: HarperCollins, 2012.

Foster, Charles. *What Do I Do Now?* New York: Simon & Schuster, 2001.

Foster, Richard N. *Innovation, The Attackers Advantage.* New York: Summit Books, 1986.

Frei, Frances and Morriss, Anne. *Uncommon Service.* Boston: Harvard Business School Publishing, 2012.

Friel, John C. and Friel, Linda. *The 7 Best Things Happy Couples Do.* Deerfield Beach: Health Communications, Inc., 2002.

Freud, Sigmund. *Totem and Taboo.* Trans. A.A. Brill. New York: Vintage Books, 1946.

Fry, Ron. *101 Great Answers to the Toughest Interview Questions,* 4th Edition. Franklin Lakes: Career Press, 2000.

Gardner, Howard. *Frames of Mind.* New York: Basic Books, Inc., 1985.

Gee, Jeff and Gee, Val. *Super Service.* New York: McGraw-Hill, 1999.

Gelb, Michael J. *More Balls than Hands: Juggling Your Way to Success by Learning to Love Your Mistakes.* New York: Prentice Hall Press, 2003.

Gerstman, Bradley, Pizzo, Christopher and Seldes, Rich. *What Men Want.* New York: Harper, 2002.

Gilbert, Roberta M. *Extraordinary Relationships: A New Way of Thinking About Human Interactions.* New York: John Wiley & Sons, Inc., 1992.

Gilden, Linda J. *Love Notes on His Pillow.* Birmingham: New Hope Publishers, 2006.

Gingras, Sandy. *What A Woman Needs.* Kansas City: Andrews McMeel Publishing, LLC, 2008.

Gitomer, Jeffrey. *Customer Satisfaction is Worthless: Customer Loyalty is Priceless.* Austin: Bard Press, 1998.

Gladwell, Malcolm. *blink, The Power of Thinking without Thinking.* New York: Little, Brown and Company, 2005.

Gladwell, Malcolm. *The Tipping Point.* New York: Little, Brown and Company, 2000.

Godek, Gregory J.P. *10,000 Ways to Say I Love You.* Naperville: Casablanca Press, 1999.

Godin, Seth. *Linchpin, Are You Indispensable?* New York: The Penguin Group, 2010.

Godin, Seth. *Unleashing the Idea Virus.* Dobbs Ferry: Do You Zoom, Inc., 2000.

Goldsmith, Marshall. *What Got You Here Won't Get You There.* New York: Hyperion, 2007.

Goldstein, Noah J., Martin, Steve J. and Cialdini, Robert B. *Yes! 50 Scientifically Proven Ways to Be Persuasive.* New York: Free Press, 2008.

Gottman, John M. and DeClaire, Joan. *The Relationship Cure.* New York: Three Rivers Press, 2001.

Gottman, John M. and Silver, Nan. *The Seven Principles for Making Marriage Work.* New York: Three Rivers Press, 1999.

Goulston, Mark. *Just Listen.* New York: AMACOM, 2010.

Gray, John. *Mars and Venus in the Workplace.* New York: Harper Collins Publishers, 2002.

Gray, John. *Mars and Venus Together Forever.* New York: Harper Perennial, 1996.

Gray, John. *Men Are From Mars, Women Are From Venus.* New York: Harper Collins Publishers, 1992.

Gray, John. *Venus on Fire, Mars on Ice.* Coquitlam: Mind Publishing, 2010.

Groopman, Jerome. *How Doctors Think.* Boston: Houghton Mifflin, Co., 2008.

Greene, Bob and Fulford, D.G. *To Our Children's Children.* New York: Doubleday, 1993.

Gross, Daniel. *Greatest Business Stories of All Time.* Ed. Editors of Forbes Magazine. New York: John Wiley & Sons, Inc.,1996.

Gross, Ronald. *Socrates' Way.* New York: Tarcher/Putnam, 2002

Gunther, Randi. *Relationship Saboteurs.* Oakland: New Harbinger Publications, 2010.

Hall, Edward T. *The Hidden Dimension.* Garden City: Anchor Press/Doubleday, 1969.

Hall, Edward T. *The Silent Language.* Garden City: Anchor Press/Doubleday, 1973.

Haltzman, Scott and Theresa Foy Digeronimo. *The Secrets of Happily Married Men.* San Francisco: Jossey-Bass, 2006.

Haltzman, Scott and Theresa Foy Digeronimo. *The Secrets of Happily Married Women.* San Francisco: Jossey-Bass, 2009.

Haltzman, Scott and Theresa Foy Digeronimo. *The Secrets of Happy Families.* San Francisco: Jossey-Bass, 2009.

Harkavy, Daniel. *Becoming a Coaching Leader.* Nashville: Thomas Nelson, Inc., 2007.

Harvey, Christine. *Secrets of the World's Top Sales Performers.* Holbrook: Bob Adams Publishers, Inc., 1990.

Hawken, Paul. *Growing a Business.* New York: Fireside, 1987.

Higgins, James M. *101 Creative Problem Solving Techniques.* Winter Park: New Management Publishing Co., 1994.

Hill, Napoleon. *Law of Success:* The 21st Century Edition. Ed. Ann Hartley and Bill Hartley. Los Angeles: Highroads Media, 2004.

Hill, Napoleon *Think and Grow Rich!.* Ed. Ross Cornwell. San Diego: Avantine Press, 2004.

Horn, Sam. *Tongue Fu!: How to Deflect, Disarm, and Defuse Any Verbal Conflict.* New York: St. Martin's Griffin, 1996.

Hsieh, Tony. *Delivering Happiness: A Path to Profits, Passion and Purpose.* New York: Business Plus, 2010.

Inghilleri, Leonardo and Solomon, Micah. *Exceptional Service Exceptional Profit.* New York: AMACOM, 2010.

Jaynes, Sharon. *Becoming the Woman of His Dreams.* Eugene: Harvest House Publishers, 2005.

Jones, Fances Cole. *How to Wow.* New York: Ballantine Books, 2008.

Jones, Merry Bloch. *"I Love Him, But..."* New York: Workman Publishing, 1995.

Jones, Robert Llewellyn. *"I Love Her, But..."* New York: Workman Publishing, 1996.

Kay, Beverly and Jordan-Evans, Sharon. *Love 'Em or Lose 'Em: Getting Good People to Stay.* San Francisco: Berrett-Koehler Publishers, Inc.,1999.

Keirsey, David. *Please Understand Me II, Temperament, Character, Intelligence.* Del Mar: Nemesis Book Co., 1998.

Kiam, Victor. *Going For It!, How to Succeed As an Entrepreneur.* New York: Signet, 1986.

Leahy, Monica Mendez. *1001 Questions to Ask Before You Get Married.* New York: McGraw Hill, 2004.

Leeds, Dorothy. *The 7 Powers of Questions.* New York: Perigree, 2000.

Leland, Karen and Bailey, Keith. *Customer Service for Dummies* 2nd Edition. New York: Wiley Publishing, Inc., 1999.

MacGregor, Cynthia, and Bobb, Vic. *The I Love You Book.* Berkeley: Conari Press, 2002.

Mackay, Harvey. *Swim With the Sharks.* New York: William Morrow & Co., 1988.

Marshall, Bethany. *Deal Breakers.* New York: Simon Spotlight Entertainment, 2007.

Maslow, Abraham H. *Toward a Psychology of Being.* New York: D. Van Nostrand Company, 1968.

McCormack, Mark H. *Never Wrestle With a Pig.* New York: Penguin Books, 2000.

McCormack, Mark H. *What They Don't Teach You at Harvard Business School.* New York: Bantam Books, 1984.

McGinnis, Alan Loy. *The Friendship Factor: How to Get Closer to the People You Care For.* Minneapolis: Augsburg Books, 2004.

McLuhan, Marshall. *Understanding Media: The Extension of Man.* New York: Signet, 1964.

Moore, Thomas. *Care of the Soul.* New York: HarperCollins Publishers,1992.

Maurer, Robert. *The Kaizen Way: One Small Step Can Change Your Life.* New York: Workman Publishing. 2004.

Maxwell, John C. *Failing Forward.* Nashville: Thomas Nelson, Inc. 2003.

Maxwell, John C. *The 17 Indisputable Laws of Teamwork Workbook.* Nashville: Thomas Nelson Publishers, 2003.

Maxwell, John C. *The 21 Indispensable Qualities of a Leader.* Nashville: Thomas Nelson Publishers, 1999.

Maxwell, John C. *The 21 Irrefutable Laws of Leadership Workbook.* Nashville: Thomas Nelson Publishers, 2002.

Maxwell, John C. *Developing the Leaders Around You.* Nashville: Thomas Nelson Publishers. 1995.

Maxwell, John C. *The Winning Attitude. Developing the Leaders Around You. Becoming a Person of Influence.* Nashville: Thomas Nelson Publishers, 2003. Three Books in One Volume

Maxwell, John C. *Thinking for a Change.* New York: Warner Business Books, 2003.

McCormack, John and Legge, David R. *Self-Made in America*. Reading: Addison-Wesley Publishing, Co., 1990.

McKay, Matthew, Fanning, Patrick and Paleg, Kim. *Couple Skills*. Oakland: New Harbinger Publications, Inc., 1994.

McTigue, G. Gaynor. *Life's Little Frustration Book*. New York: St. Martin's Press, 1994.

Mindell, Phyllis. *A Woman's Guide to the Language of Success*. Englewood Cliffs: Prentice Hall, 1995.

Mitchell, Donald and Coles, Carol. *The Ultimate Competitive Advantage*. San Francisco: Berrett-Koehler Publishers, Inc., 2003.

Morelan, Bill. *Married for Life, Inspirations from Those Married 50 Years or More*. Kansas City: Hallmark, 2004.

Morrison, Terri, Conaway, Wayne A., and Borden, George A. *Kiss, Bow or Shake Hands*. Holbrook: Adams Media Corporation, 1994.

Murphy, John. *The How of Wow!: Secrets Behind World Class Service*. Naperville: Simple Truths, LLC., 2012.

Nalebuff, Barry and Ayres, Ian. *Why Not? How to Use Everyday Ingenuity to Solve Problems Big and Small*. Boston: Harvard Business School Press, 2004.

Neal Jr., James E. *Effective Phrases for Performance Appraisals*. Perrysburg: Neal Publications, Inc., 2000.

Newman, John. *How to Stay Cool, Calm & Collected*. New York: AMACOM, 1992.

Nierenberg, Gerard I., and Calero, Henry H. *How to Read a Person Like a Book*. New York: Pocket Books, 1971.

O'Connor, Peter. *Understanding Jung, Understanding Yourself*. New York: Paulist Press, 1985.

Orfalea, Paul and Marsh, Ann. *Copy This!* New York: Workman Publishing, 2005.

Ounce of Prevention: *Short Stories to Keep your Marriage Healthy and Happy.* Comp. The National Healthy Marriage Institute, 2008.

Page, Susan. *How One of You Can Bring the Two of You Together.* New York: Broadway Books, 1997.

Papadopoulos, Linda. *What Men Say, What Women Hear.* New York: Simon Spotlight Entertainment, 2009.

Pausch, Randy. *The Last Lecture.* New York: Hyperion, 2008.

Qubein, Nido R. *Seven Choices for Success and Significance: How to Live Life From the Inside Out.* Naperville: Simple Truths, LLC, 2011.

Quindlen, Anna. *A Short Guide to a Happy Life.* New York: Random House, 2000.

Ritter, Al. *The 100/0 Principle: The Secret of Great Relationships.* Naperville: Simple Truths, LLC, 2010.

Robinson, Jonathan. *Communication Miracles for Couples.* San Francisco: Conari Press, 1997.

Rogers, Fred. *Many Ways to Say I Love You.* New York: Hyperion, 2006.

Schiffman, Stephan. *The 25 Sales Habits of Highly Successful Salespeople.* Avon: Adams Media Corporation, 1994.

Schultz, Howard and Yang, Dori Jones. *Pour Your Heart Into It.* New York: Hyperion, 1997.

Seligman, Martin E.P. *Flourish.* New York: Free Press. 2011.

Settle, Robert B. and Alreck, Pamela L. *Why They Buy: American Consumers Inside and Out.* New York: John Wiley & Sons, Inc., 1986.

Sewell, Carl and Brown, Paul B. *Customers for Life.* New York: Doubleday, 2002.

Shepard, Aaron. *Aiming at Amazon.* Friday Harbor: Shepard Publications, 2009.

Siler, Todd. *Think Like a Genius.* New York: Bantam Books, 1996.

Silverstein, Michael J. *Treasure Hunt: Inside the Mind of the Consumer.* New York: Penguin Group, 2006.

Simmons, Annette. *The Story Factor: Inspiration, Influence, and Persuasion Through the Art of Storytelling.* New York: Perseus Books Group, 2001.

Simon, Hermann. *Hidden Champions, Lessons from 500 of the World's Best Unknown Companies.* Boston: Harvard Business School Press, 1996.

Sobel, Andrew and Panas, Jerold. *Power Questions.* Hoboken: Wiley & Sons, Inc., 2012.

Spencer, Miles and Ennico, Cliff. *27 Rules for Creating and Growing a Breakaway Business.* New York: HarperCollins, 1999.

Sternberg, Robert J. *Love Is a Story: A New Theory of Relationships.* New York: Oxford University Press, Inc., 1998.

Stoltzfus, Tony. *Coaching Questions, A Coach's Guide to Powerful Asking Skills.* Virginia Beach: Tony Stoltzfus, 2008.

Stoltzfus, Tony. *Leadership Coaching.* Virginia Beach: Tony Stoltzfus, 2005.

Strauss, Steven E. *The Business Start-up Kit.* Chicago: Dearborn Trade Publishing, 2003.

Stross, Randall E., *e Boys.* New York: Crown Publishers, 2000.

Ury, William. *Getting Past No, Negotiating with Difficult People.* New York: Bantam Books, 1991.

Valenti, Jessica. *He's a Stud, She's a Slut and 49 Other Double Standards Every Woman Should Know.* Berkeley: Seal Press, 2008.

Vamos, Mark N. and Lidsky, David. *Fast Company's Greatest Hits: Ten Years of the Most Innovative Ideas in Business.* New York: Penguin Group, 2006.

Vise, David A. and Malseed, Mark. *The Google Story.* New York: Delacorte Press, 2005.

Vitale, Joe. *There's a Customer Born Every Minute.* Hoboken: John Wiley

& Sons, Inc. 2006.

Von Oech, Roger. *A Whack on the Side of the Head*. New York, Warner Books, 1983.

Wachtel, Ellen. *We Love Each Other, But...* New York: St. Martin's Griffin, 1999.

Wagner, Rodd and Muller, Gale. *Power of 2*. New York: Gallup Press, 2009.

Wagoner, Kathy. *The Promise of Friendship*. Naperville: Sourcebooks, Inc., 2002.

Waite, Linda J. and Gallagher, Maggie. *The Case for Marriage*. New York: Broadway Books, 2000.

Walser, Robyn D. and Westrup, Darrah. *The Mindful Couple*. Oakland: New Harbinger Publications, Inc., 2009.

Webster, Bryce. *The Power of Consultative Selling*. Paramus: Prentice Hall, 1987.

Weiner-Davis, Michele. *Change Your Life and Everyone In it*. New York: Fireside, 1995.

Weiner-Davis, Michele. *Divorce Busting*. New York: Simon & Schuster, 1992.

Weiner-Davis, Michele. *Getting Through to the Man You Love*. New York: St. Martin's Griffin, 1998.

Weiner-Davis, Michele. *The Sex-Starved Marriage*. New York: Simon and Schuster Paperbacks, 2003.

Williams, Jeff and Williams, Jill. *Marriage Coaching*. Springfield: Grace & Truth Relationship Education, LLC, 2011.

Wilber, Ken. *A Brief History of Everything*. Boston: Shambhala Publications, 2000.

Yamada, Haru. *Different Games, Different Rules*. New York: Oxford Press, 1997.

Yager, Jan. *When Friendship Hurts.* New York: Fireside, 2002.

Young, Rodney. *Five-Minute Lessons in Successful Selling.* Engle-wood-Cliffs: Prentice-Hall, Inc., 1985.